High Bottom

Letting Go of Vodka & Chardonnay

Tammy Roth

Wandering in the Words Press

Cover Art by Tammy Roth
Author photo by Gabriela Aguirre-Iriarte

This is a memoir and contains some autobiographical elements about the author. The author has made every attempt to recreate events, locales, and conversations from her memories of them. In order to maintain their anonymity, the author may have changed or may have left out the names of individuals, places, and identifying characteristics and details such as physical properties, occupations, and places of residence.

This book is not intended as a substitute for the medical advice of a physician. The reader should regularly consult a physician in matters relating to his/her health and particularly with respect to any symptoms that may require diagnosis or medical attention.

PUBLISHED BY WANDERING IN THE WORDS PRESS
February 2016

ISBN-10: 0-9967878-3-6
ISBN-13: 978-0-9967878-3-3

Second Edition

For Doc

I WAS A PARTY GIRL

I am sitting in a Pacific beachfront home with some of my favorite women in the world. They are sipping red wine, and I have no desire for it. This is a miracle.

A few years prior, I got sober. Back then, I would have never believed that I could be enjoying myself in such a perfect setting for overindulgence and not be tempted. Not only does alcohol no longer entice me, but also, now you couldn't pay me to drink. At this point it's poison to my body and poison to my soul.

Among us, we have a 30-year range in age. The group includes a young yogini, an author, two women I've known since graduate school and two others I know from various women's groups. The sun sets over the ocean as we place a meal of grilled salmon and a colorful salad filled with bright red strawberries and toasted almonds on the table. Kimberly is asking Tiina about her Finnish accent and the double "I"s in her name. She pours a bottle of red into five glasses. I notice she only fills them about one-third of the way. I can't help but observe. Even though I have no desire for the wine, I still find myself acting the role of the alcohol police.

I'm not tempted, but I am cautious and alert. Alcohol raises a bit of anxiety in me now. I have gotten so used to being a non-drinker that I hadn't even considered there might be drinking on this getaway. I had my first pang of anxiety while we were shopping for groceries and I noticed Merrill and Kimberly exploring the wine aisle. I took a few deep breaths, but I knew that I would be okay.

Outside, the blazing sunset casts an orange and purple sheen on the breaking waves. I pick up a faint scent of the wine. Even though it's not a cheap bottle, a hint of vinegar catches in my nostrils. It reminds me of ferocious hangovers.

I can't help but watch them and their glasses. I am highly intrigued by normal drinkers. I used to dream of being one. The other women sip their wine, splitting only one bottle between the five of them. In my drinking days, I would have viewed one bottle of wine as an insult. I would have considered not even drinking. *What's the use if I can have only a few sips?*

It is the first night of our getaway. I know all of the women, but they don't know each other. I am the common link between them, and I steer conversation toward discovering their similarities and connections. One commonality screams at me. Each of them has a normal relationship with alcohol. I do not. My sudden preoccupation with their drinking habits reminds me of all the wasted time and energy I spent thinking about alcohol.

Without it in my life, I'm filled with clarity and energy. I love waking before the alarm with a clear head and feeling excited about my day. My life is peaceful and filled with a calming meditation and yoga practice. I'm creative. I paint and write. I go on retreats and connect with others on a deep level. I read stacks of books and actually comprehend as well as finish them. I have a community of recovering friends. I have tapped into the mystical and greet each day with curiosity about what synchronistic events await me.

I spent years wondering if I had a problem. I spent years waking up to a pounding head full of regret. Each blinding pulse in my temples flashed faint memories of behaving inappropriately, talking too much and too loudly, being crass, flirting and sometimes acting rude. I always wondered what I had said and done the night before—or worse, wondered what I couldn't remember about the night before. I was a party girl.

Being a party girl in your 20s has its benefits and holds a certain amount of intrigue. In your 40s, though, it means dehydrated skin and a flood of self-loathing, anxiety and depression. Not so sexy.

In the first stages of sobriety, I had regret. Why hadn't I reigned myself in at 30? Even 35. If I had, then I would have ended up a "normal" middle-aged drinker like these women. I'd be able to enjoy just one-third of a glass of wine. But now I view recovery as one of the best things that has ever happened in my life. Who am I kidding? I never had a normal relationship with alcohol to begin with. It was a fiery, passionate love affair from the first sip. And we all know those types of liaisons involve a lot of drama.

For years, I knew alcohol was not good for me. And morning after morning, I vowed to change. I was on a perpetual plan to better manage the drinking, but I did not consider that I would ever give it up. The plan was always to cut back. Not spend so much time together. I would think I was in control of the relationship, but in reality, alcohol ruled my life and would give me just enough space to believe I was okay. I was in denial.

Every few weeks, I would wake up nursing my throbbing head and inevitably vomit to make myself feel better. Then I would swear to myself, "Never again!" I would be a responsible drinker. If I drank and didn't have a hangover, I viewed that as an achievement. I would be responsible for a few weeks at a time—sometimes even longer. And I would feel like I had taken control. Then I'd slip up. Alcohol and I would have an intense date. These dates were never planned. They were more of an "I-was-on-your-side-of-town-and-thought-I-would-drop-in" kind of situation.

The 20-something "party girl" I once was had grown up into a "have-a-drink-every-night woman." The reasons ran the gamut. I deserved it. I need to relax. I do really stressful work. It's Thursday! There was always a justification. Some nights were fine, two glasses of wine—just enough to take the edge off. But many were over the top.

I'M NOT THE CRYING TYPE

In the recovery world there's a term called hitting bottom. For many, this involves losing something big like a spouse, job, house, kids, reputation, etc. Perhaps the lowest point is receiving an orange jumpsuit after the highway patrol has found you driving in the wrong direction on the freeway. Or when you wake up in another city in another state and have no recollection of how you got there.

I did not experience a defining rock-bottom moment. I hadn't been caught drinking and driving, my husband was not giving me any ultimatums, and no one had even suggested I might have a problem with alcohol. But I did feel like I was starting to lose my mind. Self-loathing and depression had taken hold. I could barely stand to look at myself in the mirror. I used alcohol to escape myself, which only made me feel worse. I longed to awaken to a new life before the old life killed me. My trifecta of self-loathing, anxiety and depression was a lethal combination. I was quickly losing interest in living. I've since learned that, generally speaking, alcoholics are seekers and need meaning in their lives. I had very little. Even though my life was filled with success and plenty of positive things, I was lacking a deep sense of purpose, connection and meaning.

I didn't crash my car, and my liver wasn't failing, but an important event did provide a catalyst for me to reexamine my life. A friend committed suicide. Her death triggered a mass amount of anxiety and a slew of questions. Suddenly I found myself looking at the programming that lived within my DNA. Fear, control, co-dependence, inadequacy, and shame lived in my cells. Her suicide really stirred up my own cellular soup. It made me come face to face with all of my ducking and drinking to avoid feeling any of the previously mentioned.

I have always had an exit strategy for everything in my life. Jobs, marriages, friendships—I could terminate these things easily. I had walked out of a marriage with barely a conversation about my dissatisfaction. I went to work on a Monday morning and never came home. My husband at the time was shocked to say the least. I also had a pattern of leaving jobs without a shred of sentiment. When I was done, I was done. I wouldn't email, call or return for lunch with the gang, even if I'd had a strong relationship with my co-workers. I had never been willing to face the emotionally uncomfortable challenges in life. Bolting had always been the answer.

In fact, I had subconsciously been counting on suicide as the ultimate plan B. If things got *too* uncomfortable, I would just check out. I never had a concrete plan, and I never seriously considered it, but it was always there. However, my friend's choice to end her life suddenly challenged my coping strategy. I had been out for drinks with her on Thursday, and she was dead by Sunday. She had a husband, a child, parents. Her decision changed their entire lives. Nothing would ever be the same for any of them.

Suicide had previously appeared to me as some kind of lofty, dream-like escape route. But now it had become absolutely fucking real. And painful. For me, it would no longer be an option. I would have to learn to face challenges, live life, surrender and allow myself to be vulnerable.

The night I heard the news was the turning point for me. My husband was out of town, and I was home alone. I read about her death in an email. The words on the page made me feel incredibly vulnerable, raw and scared. My ultimate coping strategy had been ripped from me. I was faced with the reality that I had to learn to fully live life. But I didn't know how to do it. I was scared of what I might have to learn. My decision to explore what I was feeling rather than to dive into a bottle of chardonnay was a big step toward a new life. However, another year would pass before I would actually quit drinking.

Rather than cozying up with my somewhat reliable alcohol, I chose to meditate on what was bubbling inside. Meditation was a normal part of my routine. I had taken a primordial sound meditation class a few years before and had really connected with having a mantra. I had a daily practice. It calmed me. It didn't stop me from drinking, but perhaps it slowed my progression. Who knows?

On this particular night, I chose a different meditation route. Rather than focusing on my mantra, I allowed my feelings to come to the surface. Dark, heavy fear constricted my chest. I acknowledged it. I sat with it. I listened to what it had to tell me. But, I couldn't hear anything. Instead, I cried. Deep, gasping, ridiculously dramatic sobs. I'm not the crying type. Something had taken over my body. There were so many years of repressed emotions packed solid into my being; the only way to begin dislodging them was with a violent crying purge. I felt the darkness release, and I felt relief. Yet I knew I had work to do.

YOUR ROOTS ARE SHOWING

I come from a firm stock of determined women. My grandparents were poor farmers who eventually made a solid life for themselves. But in the beginning, they worked hard, and my petite grandmother did everything a man could do, from chopping tobacco and milking cows to drowning newborn kittens when there were too many mouths to feed. I'm guessing that's one way emotions start getting repressed. For them, every action was about endurance rather than examining feelings and life purpose.

My mother was an only child, and her hard working parents pretty much left her to her own devices from infancy. They would put her in a basket in a shady spot of the field as they went about their work for the day. It wasn't neglect; it was survival. As she grew older, she made playmates out of the cats, dogs, mice and dirt. She was thrilled when she finally started classes. It opened up a whole new world for her. In high school, she became a cheerleader, joined 4-H and started the county's first girl's softball league. She also met my father.

She and Dad fell crazy in love. So in order to guarantee themselves a shot at spending the rest of their lives together, she got pregnant. She was only 15 years old, and he was 17. They got married. That decision took a lot of courage and determination. There were so many other possible outcomes, but they stuck it out and stayed married for 17 years. It was proof that there was tenacity flowing in the amniotic fluid of my beginning.

My parents moved into an apartment near the town square in Elkton, Kentucky. Ed and Grace, my maternal grandparents, paid their rent at $25 a month. At first, Mom and Dad didn't tell anyone they were married. They knew they would be kicked out of school. Eventually, the principal found out and expelled them. My mother gave up her dream of going to college and becoming a schoolteacher.

I was born on a Friday at midnight, and the doctor was drunk. Mom and Grace both knew he was drunk, but what could they do in a tiny little town in Kentucky at midnight? Even drunk, he was the best option they had. The doctor left internal sutures in Mom and stitched her back up. This caused infection to set in. She became sick, and I became ill from nursing. It was a rocky beginning.

Mom and Dad moved into a trailer that sat in the front yard of Ed and Grace's house. Mom was afraid to be alone while Dad worked the midnight shift at the factory. She often hid us in the closet. There was nothing to be afraid of. The only things lurking out the back door were animals. We always had a plethora of kittens and puppies. A white fence behind the farmhouse contained Big Jim, a huge chestnut horse who would eat sugar cubes out of my hand. Behind gated pastures roamed a few Hereford and Charolais along with—at the right time of the year—plenty of calves.

Ed and Grace adored me—and my little brother, too, after he came along. They were early rising, country people who got up before dawn and ate a hearty breakfast. They used the same two heavy glass mugs every day, letting the coffee stains build up over the years. On the mornings after I had stayed the night, they stirred their coffee with extra vigor. The clanging echoed through the tiny house, making it impossible to continue sleeping. When I entered the kitchen, squinting my eyes at the approaching morning light, they would both laugh. And my grandfather would raucously greet me with, "Mornin' Sunshine!"

They lived simply and with an emotional lightness. They had the gift of finding the absurdity in most things and used humor to aid in the direst of situations. For example, Grace was involved in a life-threatening car wreck in which two young brothers broadsided her in their two-ton cattle truck. Their last name was Moomaw. Her wounds had barely started to heal when she was already laughing at the stark reality of being hit by a cattle truck filled with two Moomaws. Ed and Grace still had that spark of attraction and chemistry between them. They had mutual respect and admiration for each other and operated as equals. Their household was also filled with structure and rules, along with consequences if those rules weren't followed. There was no disrespecting or sassing. I knew to get up early and help with whatever needed to be done. I'm not sure what the consequences would have been for me, but I saw my rebellious little brother get taken into the bathroom for a spanking with a hairbrush more than once. I never experienced the consequences because I was airtight in my ability to be a "good girl" at an early age. I knew what to expect at their house, and there were never surprises. This was comforting.

Conversely, my other grandparents, Woodrow and Mamie, were mean. Mamie doled out love and attention sparingly to her five children—even in their adulthood. This kept her children in constant competition for her approval, and Mamie added fuel to the family fire by whispering fabrications and exaggerations to each of them about the others. She made fun of people constantly. She laughed at me for being fat and made fun of me for reading books. Looking back, I can see that it was incredibly juvenile behavior. She must have been a miserable person. I can only imagine the tragic childhood she had endured. I assume that had to be the reason for her cruelty toward the people who were closest to her. Mamie filled the family with deceit, fear and competition for love. Woodrow was passive and simply went along with whatever Mamie had conjured. He didn't seem to be a mean person, but I deemed him guilty by association. When I had to visit these grandparents, I felt only anxiety. I have no happy thoughts or memories of them, but I do remember the soft pink of mimosa trees, the scent of the pines, and the delicious cherry preserves that Mamie made each summer. Mother Nature provided comfort, since my grandmother didn't have the capacity.

When Mamaw Grace was young, she decided that she might outlive Ed. She knew she didn't want to depend on farming to survive. She went to beauty school, became a beautician, and opened Grace's Beauty Shoppe on the town square. She ran the beauty shop for 37 years without ever raising the price of haircuts from $2. I loved being at the beauty shop and learned to wash hair as soon as I could reach the shampoo bowl. I would check to make sure the silver-haired ladies were dry, and, if not, I would give them another 10 minutes under the seafoam green vinyl hair dryer. I'd take out the still warm rollers and throw the silver clippies into a plastic jug. I listened to the stories, the laughs and the tears of the women who had been coming to the beauty shop for years and years. Many of them dropped by every day on their lunch hour. Grace's Beauty Shoppe is where I learned about community and the power of a circle of women. Years later when I discovered my love of facilitating women's groups and the power of connection, I reflected on how the seeds had been planted in my early years amongst the fumes of Aqua Net hairspray and permanent wave solution.

My "good grandparents" weren't perfect by any means. Ed liked to binge drink. He was a hard working farmer and cattle dealer. He had a boisterous laugh and no enemies. He would go several weeks without drinking and then decide to tie one on. It wasn't too disruptive, at least not from my perspective, because I rarely saw him drunk.

In later years, I found out that Grace would call Mom and warn her that Ed had been drinking so that we wouldn't come around. I only saw him drunk a couple of times in my life, and that was only briefly because Mom had us do a 180 turn at the door the minute she saw his loose body language.

He was sloppy and slurring. He typically took pride in his western wear, from his Stetson hat down to his Dan Post boots. But after a bout of drinking, he'd lose the hat, revealing mussed up hair. His belly would hang out of his Wrangler shirt, and he'd pad around in sock feet. His cowboy persona would get lost in a case of Pabst Blue Ribbon. Everyone just stayed away and let him do his thing. Occasionally, he would wander into town, but the law knew and respected him so they'd make sure he returned home safely and without consequences. This was my limited exposure to the effects of alcohol. I didn't grow up observing family or friends partaking in cocktail hour, enjoying a beer at the lake, or even a glass of wine with dinner. Instead, teetotalers surrounded me. My only exposure to drinking was the rare glimpse of Edward on a binge.

Mom and Dad told me I was getting a baby brother or sister, when I was 3. As we were driving to the "other" grandparents' house for Thanksgiving, they coached me to go in and make the announcement. I walked inside first and belted out the good news. Mamie totally ignored me, and the rest of the clan looked to her for what their response should be. They followed her lead. For the entire nine months of my mother's pregnancy with my brother, her in-laws ignored her. No one acknowledged she was pregnant, asked when she was due, how she felt, or anything of the sort. None of them showed up at the hospital when he was born.

When Jeffrey arrived, there was a lot of tension in our tiny home. Dear brother Jeff demanded a lot of attention. I'm convinced having half your family ignore your existence can set you up for making demands right out of the shoot. Jeff never slept, and he cried constantly. As for me, I got a crash course in being low maintenance.

The doctor couldn't figure out what was wrong with him. Nothing soothed him. He refused to sleep. He didn't just cry; he wailed. It was horrendous to hear and see. One of my first memories is seeing the doctor prescribe a shot of whisky for Jeffrey's bottle. I find it ironic that I'm the alcoholic instead of him.

My dad, who was then all of 22, was responsible for financially supporting a wife and two children. I'm assuming he felt a lot of internal and external pressure. I've come to believe that just by remaining in the picture and not bolting as fast as he could, he did far more than most of the male population would do at 22 years old. My mom was only 20, so any dreams of education, career or anything—besides raising two kids—went out the window.

I now have a lot of compassion for my parents. I know the early years of marriage are a real challenge. Throwing babies into the mix increases the challenge, and being so young that the pre-frontal lobes of the brain haven't fully developed seems like a real recipe for disaster. Plus, Dad came from a household of dysfunction, and Mom came from one of alcoholism. I think they each needed a summer away at Outward Bound more than they needed a spouse and babies. But things were different in the '60s in Kentucky, and they bucked up and did what they needed to do.

After Jeff's birth, my dad left the factory and became a deliveryman for the Colonial Bread Company. We moved to Hopkinsville. He started his route at 4 a.m., delivering loaves of bread, cakes, and pies to grocery stores. This was a lot to add to his already growing list of life stresses. He was always exhausted, and he, like my younger brother, needed a lot of soothing. I, on the other hand, was becoming very proficient at not needing anything. I'm sure Mom was relieved to see how self-sufficient I was, because she had little attention, time or energy leftover.

This was the 1960s when it was expected that children were to be seen and not heard, so it behooved me to begin my lifelong pursuit of being invisible. One only needs to watch an episode of *Mad Men* to see that children were treated much differently in that era.

My dad's brother, JR, created additional stress. He was a constant threat to everyone. JR was drafted in the '60s, but the military absolved him of his duties due to a psychiatric discharge. Supposedly, while he was in boot camp, he would wet the bed at night; then, during training, he'd stand in front of live weapons. After his discharge, he bragged about pulling one over on the government. He'd receive government and V.A. assistance for the rest of his life.

JR had stolen my dad's first paycheck. Dad had earned it after working the entire summer in a tobacco patch when he was 15. Woodrow and Mamie did nothing. The theft continued. After Mom and Dad married, they had opened a checking account. JR stole blanks and used them to write bad checks. Rather than pressing charges, the small-town bank left it up to the family to sort it out.

The local rumors were that JR was involved in drug and car theft rings backed by the mafia. Once, after my dad had been promoted to supervisor at the bread company and had to make the nightly deposit of cash, JR went so far as to arrange an armed robbery of him. He bragged about it later.

JR was a con artist. He was flashy and charismatic. He upped the ante when he married Pat, a beautiful blonde. Together, they were a powerful pair. She liked to brag about their antics. She told stories of going into jewelry stores and looking at loose diamonds. While JR distracted the workers, she would swallow the diamonds. Twice, my parents had to make a run to Florida to bail them out of jail and get their kids out of foster care.

However, JR felt threatened by Pat. She was the smarter of the two. He shot and killed her in the house while their two children were present. As usual, JR escaped severe consequences and only had to serve seven years in a psychiatric facility.

It's not that we spent that much time with JR, but he exemplifies how dysfunctional my father's side of the family was. And we did spend a lot of time with them. Having the safety, security and structure of the good grandparents highlighted the volatility of the bad grandparents. I didn't have the words to explain how I felt as a child, but I do know that being around them scared me and sometimes made me physically ill with nausea, stomach pain and vomiting.

AND A SIDE ORDER OF FRIES

We moved to the big city of Nashville when I was in grade school. I watched the news. I heard about all of the crime. I was scared. I saw things, too. A home on our street had a faulty gas water heater, and the entire house blew up. I was terrified the same would happen to us. But I never voiced my fears. I kept them locked tightly away. I fell asleep each night with a running mantra asking to be safe through the night. Around this age I was also getting indoctrinated at Sunday School and church with the fear-of-God mentality. I prayed for God to keep me safe, but I also feared that I might have sinned too much to deserve being protected. My fear really got juiced up when a 9-year-old girl scout was abducted and killed while selling cookies. I was 9. I was a girl scout. I watched this on the news but still never voiced any of my concerns.

Looking back, I know I was loved, but considering my parents' rocky start, I don't believe they were capable of creating a sense of emotional security in our home, most likely because they couldn't feel it themselves.

We didn't talk about fear—or any feelings for that matter—in our family, and my mom reserved the nurturing and affection for my father. Keeping him calm was her way of protecting me. I felt responsible for helping her maintain the peace in our home. I learned to be self-sufficient and invisible. And I learned to not make waves. I never broke rules, I went to bed when I was supposed to and I always hopped up right before the alarm went off. I was a good girl. I learned to cook and clean and help take care of the house.

I even found ways to soothe my nervousness. I started overeating and gaining weight around age 7. I would eat two cheeseburgers and loads of fries every Friday night before watching the *Brady Bunch*. I ate as much as a grown man. Plus, Dad would bring home day-old cherry turnovers, pecan swirls and honey buns. On Saturday mornings I'd heat up honey buns in a skillet full of butter and watch cartoons while swigging chocolate milk.

Mom tiptoed around, trying hard to please both Dad and my brother. Jeff was a live wire who created a lot of chaos. It's interesting how our early development affected both Jeff and me, yet how it played out differently in our adult personalities. He has always been a charismatic, outgoing, successful salesman, demanding what he needs and getting it. I, on the other hand, continue to focus inward, remain stoic and view asking for help as weak or needy. However, I've worked hard to change my approach.

Mom tried to control my little Tasmanian devil of a brother so that he wouldn't rile up Dad's anger. She did this without the help of Valium, alcohol, cigarettes or overeating. As far as I know, she had no vices. In retrospect, I think one might have come in handy.

Mom knew she didn't have to worry about me because I preferred to escape into my own world. I continued to soothe myself with food, and then I added books to the mix. I was reading novels like *Rich Man Poor Man* and *Valley of the Dolls* at the age of 9. I loved getting lost in a thick novel. I learned a lot about life through fiction that was inappropriate for a kid. The drama unfolding in the books was much more intriguing than the same old theatrics at my house. I learned about sex, drugs, and the complexities of adult relationships. When I discovered the public library and the seemingly infinite supply of stories, I felt as if I'd slipped into a clandestine world and was fortunate enough to have been given the secret code for entrance.

We moved a few more times—all within a 150-mile radius—but each move required new schools, new friends and a period of adjustment. I went to a total of eight schools in twelve years. I was fat, and it was probably fortunate that I felt invisible. I didn't get involved in after school activities. I had to take care of my brother and cook dinner. I may not have gotten much in the way of nurturing, but I did learn responsibility, basic life skills and a good work ethic. Those are tools that have served me well. I also learned to get by with few friends. I had a hard time trusting people because I'd learned quickly that I couldn't trust many family members.

My dad was very strict, and as I grew older, he became even more so. It was easier to not ask for much and not cause waves. As a pre-teen, I didn't beg to go to parties and do things that typical kids did. I knew if I asked, it would make things harder on my mom because Dad would take it out on her. I opted to stay at home in my bedroom with piles of books and magazines. I didn't talk on the phone (considering there was only one and it was hanging on the kitchen wall), and I definitely didn't have boyfriends.

I lived with the belief that Dad's anger could turn physical if I didn't keep myself in check. I never endured any actual threats, but the energy in our home had grown more and more tense over the years, and I sensed something was always about to blow. In my constant struggle to control things, I thought that I had more influence than I did. I thought that as long as I was "good" enough I might help subdue things. I grew up rigidly non-demonstrative, so later when I found my inhibitions disappearing with each sip of wine, I felt liberated in many ways.

We did fun things as a family, like going camping and vacationing at Disney World, but I was always riddled with anxiety and locked into a state of hyper vigilance. I've tried to remember happy childhood memories. I'm sure there were joyous occasions, but my memory doesn't get a hit on them. That's not because they didn't occur. Perhaps they didn't get locked into my mind. Research shows that our brains are hardwired to hold onto negative experiences with more tenacity than positive ones as a primal function to keep us safe. I now believe that I was always physically safe, but there was a lot of emotional turmoil woven into our lives, and I was highly sensitive to it. I learned to not let my guard down or enjoy the fun times because they too could turn on a dime. When I was struggling to get sober, I wondered why I self medicated. I had never experienced trauma. No, I never experienced big trauma, but we were swimming in dysfunction, fear, and insidious trauma on a daily basis.

I had a friend, Debbie, with whom I often slept overnight. I felt very fortunate to stay with her because she had what I perceived to be a very exciting life for a 10 year old. She lived with her single mom and two sisters in a town house. Her mom was very glamorous and had an evening job as a lounge singer at the downtown Sheraton. The nanny would arrive, and Debbie's mom would come out dressed in sequins or gold lamé with her long platinum hair piled high in an updo. She looked like a life-size Barbie. Debbie and I tried to stay awake to see her again when she got home. But we always fell asleep.

Who knows, Debbie may now be writing about her broken childhood with no father and an absent mother. We all have issues. That's how we learn, grow and become resilient. I don't blame my mom and dad. They were doing the best they could as young parents. They had no training, very few role models, and they definitely didn't get what they needed as kids.

RECORDS, BOOKS AND CIGARETTES

At 13 I got my first job at the Sound Shop. It was a music store that sold 45s, eight-tracks and incense. I started work, but when it came time to figure out the paperwork, my employer and I discovered that I didn't have a social security number. They weren't given at birth in the '60s. I applied for one, but it took too long to get, and the shop had to let me go because they couldn't keep me on the schedule without paying me. But I would have gladly done it for free; I loved having a job and the freedom that came with it.

During my short tenure at the Sound Shop, I started smoking cigarettes. I found this to be far more soothing than eating. I loved to smoke. My dad smoked, and I would pilfer his butts out of the ashtray when I didn't have a pack of my own. In those days, a 13 year old could buy her own cigarettes. So it was an easy addiction to acquire. I hid it from my parents, though. I would wait until the middle of the night and then I'd raise my window and hang out in the shrubs, puffing away.

I was very excited about high school. We lived in Clarksville, and I had enrolled in vocational school for cosmetology classes, as well. I would be on track to have a cosmetologist license by the time I graduated. I had a vision that I would be a hairdresser to the stars in Nashville. I have no idea where this vision came from. I wasn't necessarily familiar with country artists, and I knew nothing about Music Row. But I aspired to be something more than just a small-town shampoo girl.

Everything changed when we suddenly had to move to Paducah, Kentucky, after Dad got transferred. School had already begun for the semester, so I was a late registrant, and cosmetology classes were already full. The only vocational option left was typing and office technology. I reluctantly took the class, but I was devastated at the loss of my dream.

I felt some relief from my despair when I got a job at a pizza parlor. A fresh, new social security number allowed me a paycheck and a reward for my hard work. I worked three nights a week at Little Italy with the owner, Rose. I loved the sense of freedom that getting out of my room and out of the house gave me. I saved my money and bought my own clothes, records, books and cigarettes. Little Italy was open six nights a week, and when the other three-night girl quit, I begged Rose to give me her shifts, too. She agreed, and I worked the full six nights. I would head there straight from school. Little Italy closed at ten during the week and at midnight on the weekends. I was able to avoid the tension that was quickly escalating in my home. My parents didn't fight, but my mom continued to struggle with constantly trying to please my dad, and it wasn't working. Their dysfunctional relationship was unraveling. Thanks to my job, my self-esteem increased, and my weight decreased. I didn't allow myself to eat pizza every night. I only ate salads, and Rose let me smoke right there in the restaurant when we didn't have customers. I was getting thin as well as feeling some much needed independence.

School and homework came easily to me. Through my business classes I discovered I had quite a gift for typing. I was fast and accurate. My teacher expressed excitement at having a star typist. He signed me up for FBLA (Future Business Leaders of America) and entered me in typing contests. I won every contest I entered. I won the local, city and district contests without much effort.

I was headed to the state FBLA conference. It would be me and my IBM Selectric against the best in the state. For the first time in my life, I felt pretty special. I was the most excited I'd ever been. I couldn't imagine the freedom I would feel being out of town without parents.

The night before the trip to Lexington, I rushed to close Little Italy and haphazardly began cleaning the dough-rolling machine. It grabbed my middle finger and pulled it in between the two mechanized rollers. By the time Rose had the good sense to intervene, the machine had ground away much of the skin. Rose had to manually roll out my finger, and I had to go to the emergency room. My typing career was temporarily put on hold. And I had to miss the trip of a lifetime. I had been sure Lexington would change the trajectory of my future.

THE FIRST DIVORCE

My dad was stricter than ever. I was a teenager and not allowed to have boyfriends, talk on the phone to boys, or go to football games. But at least he let me work. And Rose let me work using only one hand while my finger grew new layers of tissue and skin.

Home became more and more volatile. My parents kept their issues quiet, so I never knew the details, but I wasn't surprised when they announced they were getting divorced. In fact, I was thrilled; I felt that I was getting divorced, too. Mom and I moved back to Clarksville. Dad remarried quickly, and my brother bounced back and forth between Dad's place and our place.

I met my first real boyfriend. My relationship with Steve was my first foray into typical adolescent freedoms. Finally, I was a normal, 15-year-old girl. Steve was 18, and he'd just graduated from high school. We fell into a serious relationship from the start. He was adopted and had his own emotional scars. With our respective wounds, we were like magnets to steel.

Mom allotted me normal teenage freedoms. I didn't abuse them, but I also didn't act like a typical teen, either. I was hyper-responsible. I moved on to another job at McDonalds. I worked full time—often until 2 a.m.—went to school and joined TOEC (Tennessee Office Education Club). My finger had grown new cells, and my typing was back up to speed, plus, I learned shorthand and how to use a Dictaphone.

Steve grew very jealous and controlling. But, I liked it. He started working at McDonald's, too. He wanted to keep an eye on me, but in my teenaged naiveté his control felt like intimacy. He demanded that I not have friends outside of our relationship or do anything without him. It was absurdly comforting.

As soon as I graduated at 17, I moved out of my mom's and rented a tiny place behind a farmhouse in Clarksville. It was a damp, dark place that sprouted mushrooms overnight in the bathtub. Each morning required mushroom harvesting before showering. I paid $125 a month in rent and began working in Nashville at a huge insurance company located in a 30-story building. I had gone from too little freedom to what was probably too much for a 17 year old. Too much felt more appropriate than too little, but I still hadn't found my "just right." I was comfortable and capable, but none of my other friends were living on their own at 17. I didn't really fit in anywhere.

I had first visited the Nashville insurance company on a field trip back in high school. I remember the elevator doors opening to the executive floor. I stared with awe at the secretary who sat behind a big wooden desk. She held a glistening glass of orange juice. Real glass, not plastic. At that moment, I set the intention that before I died or retired I would be an executive secretary. I knew I had to start on the ground floor.

I had applied to the company the day after graduation. I was eventually hired as a typist. I drove 63 miles to work and wore panty hose and high heels everyday. I believed in acting as if I already had the job I wanted. I dressed the part and acted very serious and professional. As a result, I quickly moved up the administrative ladder.

THE SECOND DIVORCE

When I turned 18, Steve and I got married, and he moved into my little farmhouse shed. But his parents eventually bought us a mobile home and put it in their side yard.. At the same time, I was growing and developing at work. The marriage and my professional path were not in alignment. I was experiencing something on this career path I'd never felt before. I was meeting new people and learning new skills. The massive company provided me with many diverse opportunities. Going to work felt very expanding. Going home felt incredibly constricting. And it's no surprise that the more expansion I experienced, the more controlling Steve became. My growth and excitement threatened him. Unfortunately, I put all of my energy into my professional growth and none of it into standing up for myself at home. I had never been one to rebel. And my mother, like many wives of the '60s and '70s, certainly hadn't been a role model for autonomy.

Most of my co-workers were women who had started at the insurance company right out of high school, as well. They were married, and their relationships sounded comparable to mine. I was in a relationship much like my parents had been, and I was surrounded by women who were in similar ones. I told myself I should be content and quit wanting. But I had a deep longing for so much more.

For starters, I just wanted to live as an adult. Steve's parents were also very controlling. They had set us up in the trailer on their land, and we all unconsciously agreed that it gave them control of us. We were their puppets. They wanted us actively involved in their church. We became Sunday school teachers and youth group leaders. We were to have a family lunch at their house each Sunday after church, and then we all went right back to church on Sunday evening. Eventually, they gave us land and helped us build a house on it. Their claws dug in deeper. I just rolled over and let it happen. Steve happily went along with it. He loved pleasing them, but I felt inner turmoil. I stifled my feelings because I figured I should just be grateful.

I longed for the simplest of things: sleeping in on a Sunday, reading the newspaper over multiple cups of coffee and rendering the possibilities the day offered. I knew small things like this would lead to far grander things that I simply couldn't yet imagine.

In those middle years of the marriage, I worked at tempering my desires. At first, I would bring them up to my co-workers. These married women, who were older than me, quickly doused my ideas. Perhaps they agreed with me about the oppression and even shared some of my wants, but the simple act of voicing my hopes for change threatened them.

During this time, I also began obsessing about my weight. I had been chunky my entire life. I had never realized I could be thin, so when I lost weight in high school, it seemed like a miracle. I joined Weight Watchers at work, and I learned a lot about how to eat healthy, but it also resulted in me assigning rules and rigidity around food and the numbers on the scale. I had begun to equate being thin with being loveable and acceptable. Having the number on the scale go down was addictive. The empty, concave feeling in my stomach was also addictive. I would often make it close to a week eating only a few hundred calories a day. I literally counted every bite that I consumed, and I felt proud when I managed to skip a meal or only eat celery, carrots or lettuce. But then a deeper hunger would catch up with me, and I would binge. I would take the first bite of something "forbidden" and I couldn't stop. And once the binge started, then I figured I had blown it, so I might as well go for it all. I would eat everything I could find in the house. Then I would feel hideous and disgusting. I wanted the mass of food out. I would attempt to purge. But, honestly, I wasn't good at purging, either. I could never quite get the technical difficulties ironed out. I was a wannabe anorexic and bulimic.

My weight bobbed up and down in a 10-pound range for several years until one day I finally tossed out the scale. Not eating and feeling rail thin was intoxicating and made me feel in control of my life. But it was such an illusion. Since being in recovery I've discovered that disordered eating patterns are typical among recovering women. I heard one woman describe recovery as whack-a-mole. You whack one addiction and another pops up.

I was an executive secretary by the time I was 21 years old. My professional lifelong goal had arrived a bit early. I was surprised at how much I could accomplish with determination, and I was ready for the next move. I studied and passed the multiple parts of the Certified Professional Secretary exam. Next, I decided to take the nine-part life insurance certification course. I was a secretary on a mission. I passed this certification program in record time. Someone asked why I had never gone to college. I'd never even considered it. No one in my family had gone to college, and no guidance counselors had talked to me about it. I had just assumed the best route for me was to start working immediately.

The company created a new department—an internal consulting group—and I was promoted. Six young MBAs—two women and four men—made up the department, and I was their administrative assistant. All six were progressive thinkers. The women were very independent, and one of them was even married and independent. This was a new world view for me. They helped me realize that my desires were normal and that I wasn't asking for much at home at all. They also helped me learn and grow in my new role. I became a sponge for new projects and opportunities.

At one point I had the opportunity to join a special project team that took me to Washington, D.C., for a month, only coming home on the weekends. I lived in an apartment complex with other team members. We explored the monuments, the parks, the Smithsonian and the history. It was fascinating. We ate dinners out, stayed up late and even went dancing. This was my first experience with social drinking. I overdid it, but everyone else did, too, so it seemed normal and exciting. I was suddenly experiencing freedom.

Each weekend I was given the option of using an airline ticket to bring someone to me, or I could go home. Steve refused to come to D.C., so I went back to Tennessee. I dreaded the weekends. I could barely wait to get back to my exciting life in the big city. On my final flight home, I cried the entire way, finding it unbearable to go back to a life with a jealous, insecure husband. But I did.

At 25 years old and with the support of my colleagues, I began considering the possibility of going to college. I was discovering that I was smarter than I had realized. Steve and I had been married for seven years, and he'd become more controlling than ever. It was no longer endearing. I wanted continued growth and I wanted him to support my growth. But he didn't like that I worked in Nashville. And now that I had these supportive co-workers, I really began questioning the marriage.

College felt like an exciting new path and a way to escape being at home. Out of pure ignorance and a strong work ethic, I enrolled in three classes to start while still working full time. I lived in Clarksville, worked in Nashville, and took college classes in Fort Campbell, Kentucky. I spent more than four hours a day on the road. I got up at 4:30 each morning to do homework, left home by 6:30, got to work early so that I could leave early and make it to class on time. I had class five evenings a week from five to ten. I'd get home by eleven to do the cooking, cleaning and laundry. I did this because Steve agreed that I could go to college as long as I kept the refrigerator full and his shirts washed and ironed. Thank goodness I had a lot of energy to go along with my strong work ethic.

But after that first semester of college, sheer exhaustion took over. Suddenly, I had very little tolerance for Steve's tyrannical rule. Not only was Steve horribly insecure and jealous, he continued to let his parents control him. Essentially, we were playing house, but his parents called all the shots. Sometimes this worked in my favor. Steve really didn't like me going to school, but his parents were fans of higher education and supported me. They told Steve to "let" me go to college.

The act of getting myself into college and actually finishing the first semester gave me great strength and courage, but my empowerment continued to threaten Steve. We had no communication skills with each other. I would occasionally sling a passive aggressive comment his way, and he would get defensive. Mostly, we just didn't communicate. I did all my talking at work. Two thirds of my life felt fulfilling, hopeful and exciting. But home life depressed me. Weekends seemed to last forever, and I looked forward to Monday mornings when I could get back into the flow of learning and growth.

Finally, I was fully leaning into this new life. And I couldn't bear the thought of spending one more minute trapped in the marriage and lifestyle I had been enduring for seven years. I considered my options. I knew that going to a marriage therapist was one choice, but it scared me. I didn't want to fix the marriage. I had outgrown it beyond a salvageable boundary. I had edged into a new field of possibility.

I had the dreaded conversation with Steve on a Saturday. He was clueless and devastated. He had thought things had been fine. He begged me to reconsider and promised me anything I wanted. We could move away from his parents. I could have friends. I could go out after work with colleagues. He would concede whatever it took. But I was beyond done.

When I left for work the following Monday morning, I told him I'd stay in a hotel for the week to gather my thoughts. That week provided the most resolve and clarity I'd ever felt in my life. I was certain I wanted a divorce, but I also agreed to go to a marriage counselor with him. We went to one session, and it helped validate that there was nothing worth saving. Steve changed the locks on the house during that week, and that really helped seal the deal for me. I know his actions were based on hurt, but his wrath made it much easier for me to leave. I never returned home after that week. I slept in on Sunday morning, read the newspaper and drank coffee until noon.

MY NEW LOVE AFFAIR

Suddenly, being a single girl in the big city felt scary. I began drinking regularly. I was guarded and introverted. So I gave alcohol a shot and discovered its remarkable power. It minimized the scary. It made me far more outgoing. I was wittier, edgier and riskier when I drank. I was fearless. An oaky chardonnay partnered well with a young divorcee living in the city. We were meant to be together.

I finally experienced adolescence at 25 years old. I had been such a responsible, hard-working teenager that I hadn't felt the typical joys and heartaches of the teen years. Steve was the only person I had ever dated. Divorce was a big exciting step, and alcohol helped me take leaps and bounds away from my marriage.

I began dating and going to nightclubs. For the most part, it was horrid. I was introverted and resented men. I didn't know how to flirt. And I had a chip on my shoulder. I was not good at being single. Dating was miserable, but at least it was different. It was new, and I felt free. Alcohol helped me loosen up and act like the 25 year old I was. But dating guys my age really didn't pan out well. Most 25 year olds were right out of college and not very responsible. I had already accumulated years of history and ambition. I didn't waste time on irresponsible or immature men. I never dated anyone for long. I got a feel for a guy pretty quickly and knew when it was time to move on. I had also tapped into my inner militant feminist. I had zero tolerance for a man trying to control me. I had a strong attitude. I actually didn't care much for men and let most of them know it.

Alcohol helped me get through those tough times, but there were plenty of signs from the start that I had a problem with it. I could never consume enough. I always wanted more and more. There were a few times I blacked out, not recalling anything that had happened after a certain point in the evening. And I always suffered hangovers. Still, the pleasure outweighed the consequences.

I created a lot of rules around drinking. Thanks to my rigid eating habits, I had become a master of discipline. In the beginning, I never drank during the week, only on the weekends. Later, I vowed to never drink and drive, and I always made sure I had a designated driver. Having these rules in place gave me the illusion of control. But like with food, I never knew when it would spiral into chaos. Somehow I was able to remain highly productive and not perceive myself as a problem drinker.

My new relationship with alcohol was volatile and confusing. I had spent my adolescence under my father's control and my early adulthood under Steve's control. I was very uptight, but more than anything, I wanted to be carefree and fun, maybe even a bit wild. I didn't know how to do it on my own. Alcohol provided a quick release from the rigidity, but I took it to the extreme. I would end up sloppy drunk and not at all like what I was shooting for. I never ceased believing I'd be able to control it better next time.

FRESH STARTS

I met Dennis about a year after the divorce. He was different. He was very, very responsible. He was 29 years old and already owned a house, a vehicle and boat. He had worked for the same company for 10 years and was about to start working for American Airlines. He was rock solid. He said what he meant and he meant what he said. He knew what he wanted in a woman and had a list of non-negotiable requirements. He had moved from St. Louis and loved Nashville and the South. He was looking for an intelligent, independent southern gal without kids and without drama. He also abhorred smoking. I loved his resolve. I met all the requirements on his list except for the last one. At the time, though, that didn't matter. I was already dating one of his friends.

It didn't take long for the relationship with the friend to fizzle. Dennis took "non-smoker" off his list of requirements, and he and I got together. Slowly. He was the exact opposite of Steve, and I was up for the challenge of learning a new way to be in a relationship.

Dennis gave me space and wanted me to grow. He supported me and never expressed jealousy. I loved the freedom, but after coming from such a controlling relationship, Dennis' lack of jealousy confused me a bit. He was very supportive of me going places, doing things and having friends. He wasn't even threatened that I had male friends. He trusted me. In my insecure moments, I felt like he didn't care enough. Rather than have a mature conversation about how I was feeling, I would stir up drama and try to start a fight. However, he typically didn't fall for my antics and wasn't going to engage in an argument. He was willing to communicate and deal with conflict, but he wasn't the fighting kind. He also wasn't the groveling kind. He was not going to try and convince me he cared enough. He simply kept showing me he cared by being honest, trustworthy and consistent. It took me years and years to trust this. His belief has always been that actions speak louder than words. He was a man of few words. But his actions spoke volumes. And most of the time, I relished being in the presence of someone with solid self worth. He didn't project his emotional needs onto me.

Dennis never mentioned anything about the fact that I smoked. He was a smart man. I would have never quit if he had asked me to. My fiery streak was still running hot, and I would never again allow a man to control me. I had tried to quit smoking many times in the past. It was such a strong addiction that I couldn't imagine ever being able to shake it. I had accepted it as a part of who I was. Plus, I knew that it would help keep me thin. But there was a deeper part of me that wanted to be free of the addiction.

One weekend Dennis and I went out of town together, and I decided to go for as long as I could without smoking. I felt more attractive when I did not smell like an ashtray. I ended up going the entire weekend without a cigarette. I decided if I could go an entire weekend, then I could quit for good. I made up my mind, and the habit actually fell away relatively fast. I was shocked. I was learning that I could do anything I set my mind to: lose weight, go to college, get a divorce, quit smoking. Yet, it would take me 20 years to give up alcohol.

Dennis and I married initially so that I would also have flight benefits and we could travel free together. We were both pretty cynical about marriage, and neither of us expected it to last until death parted us, but we were both willing to give it a shot for as long as it worked. To this day, we still have a discussion on our anniversary whether we want to renew for another year. This time around, my relationship and my professional path were very much in alignment with each other. Dennis continued to be a huge supporter of my growth and development.

I had been at the insurance company for 10 years and had done a great job climbing up the career ladder. But it was time to push on. I moved to another company the same month we married. And I soon finished my bachelor's degree. There were a lot of fresh starts. I had left my first marriage, which I had assumed would last forever. I had left the company I thought I would retire from, and I had given up an addiction I thought I would be saddled with for life.

In my new job, I was part of a company that hired 700 college graduates in a two-year period to operate the back office function of a New York bank. Suddenly, 25 year olds—who were getting a paycheck for the first time and counting the minutes until happy hour—surrounded me. Dennis worked the second shift and also worked weekend nights, so I didn't see a lot of him. I was disciplined and would work late and go to the gym on weeknights, but on the weekends while he was working I went out with friends. During this time, I appeared to drink like my companions. There were definitely nights that I had more than I should have. And there were times that I drove when I shouldn't have. The behavior didn't stand out as unusual, given my age and the crowd I was hanging out with. Considering that I had only started drinking three or four years prior, I was still in the early stages of alcohol abuse. It was such freedom to go out and have fun without worrying about how a jealous husband might react. Dennis trusted me, he supported me and he admired my drive. His encouragement and approval were intoxicating.

After working at the bank for a couple of years, I had learned quite a bit about human resource development, so I changed jobs and moved into an HR role at a road construction/rock quarry company. I spent a lot of time out in the field in small country towns wearing a hardhat and steel-toed boots. This felt very reminiscent of my roots in Kentucky. The change in work setting actually slowed my drinking a bit. The party atmosphere was gone. Instead, I worked with men who went home to their families at the end of a physically taxing day. I began drinking more at home after work.

At the same time, I decided to go to graduate school. I had only recently learned the difference between undergrad and graduate work. These were not terms that were thrown around in my childhood home, and I was just beginning to meet people who had advanced degrees. A co-worker had graduated from Vanderbilt's Human Resource Development program. I liked the sound of it, so I applied. I had no idea Vanderbilt was southern Ivy League, or else I might have shied away from trying to get in. I managed to get accepted, however, and my new company paid my way. All I had to do was work hard. I was good at that. I had intensity, focus, discipline and drive.

While growing up, no one had paid much attention to my success. No one chastised me for my failures, either. I lacked fear of failure because I had never experienced pressure to be successful. This proved to be a gift in my adulthood whenever I stretched outside of my comfort zone.

PROBLEMS BUILDING

Drinking had become very much a normal part of my life. I wasn't as active in the party lifestyle while working with the construction company as I had been at the bank, but I still built my own solid drinking practice. I never considered attending any type of social event that didn't provide access to alcohol. I typically took airplane bottles of wine into the movie theatre. I also had a drink or two at home before going to a party. I wouldn't consider dinner at a restaurant that didn't serve drinks.

I constantly planned how to work alcohol into my life, while also appearing to be in control. I did, however, make jokes and self-deprecating comments about my drinking. I assumed people would think that if I made fun of it, then I wasn't in denial, and it must not be that bad.

I spent a lot of energy on alcohol. I was working hard and putting in long hours. The harder I worked, the more drinking points I felt I had earned for my party bucket. I didn't sit at work dreaming of having a drink at lunch, but I always thought about how I might reward myself later for the hard work I was doing. If I had a particularly stressful day or I accomplished a significant task, I planned on having a drink that evening. I didn't know how to experience the full emotions of living. Instead, I chose to numb them out. I also assumed everyone else thought about alcohol all the time, too. I was shocked in my first months of sobriety to see that most people don't drink nearly as much as I thought they did.

The next two years at the road construction company were highly developmental for me. I had a sharp boss who took me under his wing and groomed me to be a leadership development specialist. I began working closely with the senior leadership team and their directives to create a middle-management leadership development program. Our department appeared to have an unlimited budget. They paid for me to go to graduate school at Vanderbilt and for any training I wanted. I had the most high-tech work tools (computers, software, and other gadgets) plus access to the company jet and helicopter for quick flights to all the field sites. It was quite a life for a naïve young woman who had not long ago left a marriage and a trailer behind in Clarksville.

My continued drinking led to another problem. I was also beginning to embarrass myself when I overindulged. My boss had put me in charge of creating and facilitating a leadership development conference. I conveniently planned it at a retreat center at a winery.

On the final night of the retreat, the wine flowed freely. Despite the fine food served, I barely touched my plate, but indulged heavily in the expensive cabernet. There were only three females at this conference and about 35 males. Even though I was coming into my power, I still had an adamant dislike for men trying to control me. These powerful male executives were the higher ups. And on a basic level, I sensed their control over me. I sat at the leadership table with them, but I knew deep down I wasn't one of them.

At dinner, I talked big and loud about an upcoming golf tournament. I boasted that I could gather a team of women golfers and win the event. In reality, I could barely golf. But I backed up my bragging with a $500 bet. The men at the table found my bravado very entertaining, and they happily accepted my wager. I dominated the conversation with my slurred proclamations. Eventually, the CEO had to calm me down. He had been sitting back in his chair appearing to enjoy the show, but I had enough awareness to recognize his body language and tone when he sat up and shifted the conversation away from me.

The next morning, I felt incredibly embarrassed, but rather than admit I had been inebriated, I continued to assert that I could pull it off. It was ridiculous. I got a team. We played. We lost. And I drank.

At another conference I organized a night out and again I drank too much. I jumped in the pool wearing my dress and pantyhose—which, I suppose, is better than jumping in the pool with nothing on. None of my antics were horribly over the top, but acting out had become the norm.

Logic should have prompted me to quit drinking at functions. But logic doesn't work with the alcoholic mind. I couldn't imagine being at these functions without alcohol. I needed the liquid courage to be socially engaging. I never planned to have more than two, but everything changed once I had that first sip. A warmth flowed through my system. It calmed me. Alcohol altered my intention, my brain chemistry and the outcome of every situation.

I had also become increasingly dissatisfied with the bureaucracy and patriarchy of my job. I had completed the masters degree and was feeling antsy and wondering, what next?

Around that time, Princess Diana died in a car wreck. I had never really followed news about the Princess before, but the accident somehow affected me. Her promising future had been ripped away. I began obsessing about her death and reading everything I could get my hands on regarding it. In hindsight, I believe she awoke within me a longing for the sacred feminine archetype. I was so immersed in a world of masculine energy. Her death seemed like a warning sign that I needed to get out of that environment. My soul was aching for a more collaborative, intuitive way of being rather than the linear, deterministic world in which I had always worked.

At this time, something prompted me to take a week off work and refinish my kitchen cabinets. It was very therapeutic. I didn't have the insight or awareness, then, to notice the symbolism of sanding down and getting to the fine wood grain and then refinishing the cabinets to their more natural state. It was hard work. I spent the entire week sanding by hand and thinking about my career path and the loss of Princess Diana. I came out of the week solid in my desire to leave the corporate path.

I felt like my soul was being sucked out of me with every hour I logged at work. I wanted to go back to school—yet again for another master's degree—to become a counselor and work for a non-profit. My new job goal had pure intentions, but I also felt the need to escape the legacy I was creating for myself. I wasn't sure how my peers perceived me. No one ever indicated I was a problem drinker. I worked incredibly hard when I wasn't playing hard. But I still felt a sense of shame and embarrassment about my drinking.

I wanted to get the hell out of the job. At the same time, I continued to count my blessings that I even had such a high-level job. I tried to cool my jets, but they wouldn't cool. I couldn't find peace. I struggled internally with my need to escape, just as I had with my first marriage.

I met with our corporate therapist, and she strongly encouraged me to find happiness within the job I had. She asserted that what I was experiencing was just life, and that I needed to "get over it," more or less. I had made my way in the corporate world and had a place at the table with the good old boys, she explained. She said that if I went back to school and started a new career path, no one would give a rat's ass about my 15 years in corporate. I would have to start fresh. I didn't totally believe this, but I made note not to have a chip on my shoulder when I entered a new field. I'd have to go into a new career with a beginner's mind. I also knew that my 15 years of experience couldn't be taken away.

Finally, I took the big step and resigned. My boss was so grateful for the work I had done in the prior two years—

with all that I had learned at Vanderbilt—that he managed to get me a year of severance pay, even though I had resigned. Instead of a drunk seeking a change of setting, I felt incredibly successful.

During my sabbatical, my former boss hired me as a consultant and paid me a generous hourly rate. The freedom of being a consultant rather than a corporate employee led to less inhibited behavior and even more drunken antics.

On one occasion, he hired me to go to Oregon for a benchmarking meeting with a leading-edge company. I drank at the airport, pounded cocktails on my flight, and then enjoyed even more in Las Vegas during my layover. In the Vegas airport, I met two other party girls who were heading to Oregon, as well. We drank together while waiting for our delayed flight. We continued to drink on the plane. By the time I landed, I could barely stand. I had already arranged for ground transportation and somehow located the driver and van to drive me the next 60 miles. I stumbled into my hotel, and when I awoke the next morning, I was as sick as I'd ever been. I couldn't hold my head up to reach the trash can. I vomited in my bed. Thankfully, there were two beds in the room and I just scooted over to the other one. I had to cancel the meeting.

I had never been this sick from drinking before. I definitely did not want to believe I had done this to myself. My denial convinced me it was viral and that having a few drinks had simply made it worse. By the second day, I felt a bit more normal, but I had missed my meeting opportunity. I headed back home. My old company paid for all of my travel expenses. And even though I had resigned, they were continuing to pay me a weekly salary. They had paid for my master's degree at Vanderbilt, and they were paying me for consulting even though I hadn't made it to the project. It was easier to stay in denial when I appeared to be so successful. I could easily rationalize away any concerns.

I still felt incredibly successful. Aside from the occasional embarrassing moment or deep shame felt during a hangover, I endured few consequences for my alcohol abuse.

I never considered that I might be an alcoholic. My image of alcoholism involved a Skid Row homeless man. My grandfather drank, but no one in my family had labeled him an alcoholic. He just went on the occasional bender. The word *alcoholism* was pretty foreign to me and definitely wasn't a word I tossed around in relation to my own issues. Yet, I had a constant feeling of needing to get myself under control. I believed my behavior was just a matter of willpower. I was confused. How could I accomplish so much with my career but not be able to keep my drinking habits in check?

GEOGRAPHIC CURE

Once I switched to the world of psychology and counseling, I wondered how my drinking habits would fit in. But surprise! It worked out just fine. Grad students like to drink, and professors sometimes join in. The difference is that they are "normal" drinkers.

Besides, after taking an addictions class, I determined I was okay. I ran all the assessments on myself. I was merely an "abuser of alcohol." I could handle that label. I rated on the low end of the scale. I was not experiencing legal issues, neglecting family responsibilities, having health problems or dealing with withdrawal symptoms. Those were things a true alcoholic experienced. "Abuser of alcohol" felt safe. Party people abused alcohol. College students abused alcohol. Most days I only had two drinks, but I didn't consider that those drinks were tall. I loved to sip out of a red solo cup.

I had the nagging feeling, though, that I might have been a bit conservative in some of my answers. For example, I didn't check the "yes" box next to, "Does alcohol interfere with your work?" The reality was that I had just left a job out of shame.

I had a series of jobs dealing with addicted and recovering populations. While in school, I worked part time teaching classes to DUI offenders. Then, for my internship, I worked with female recovering addicts in the judicial system, and I continued to work with them after graduation. Most had been in jail, had worked as prostitutes and had suffered a great deal of trauma. I was working with very severe cases of addiction. I found it easy to rationalize that I wasn't like them.

I gravitated to the counseling world of recovery while I battled my own demons. I learned a lot. Many of my co-workers were also in recovery. Some of these jobs even had the requirement upon hiring that if an applicant was in recovery, two years of sobriety were essential. When asked if I was in recovery, I always said no. The employers assumed that if I wasn't in recovery, it was because I didn't need to be. No one ever asked if I had a problem with alcohol. I frequently found myself in settings where I felt like a hypocrite.

I finished the counseling degree, got a job with a non-profit and took an 80 percent pay cut from what I had been making in the corporate world. I was valiant. I was sure the meaning and fulfillment would be worth every cent I was losing.

Instead, I actually fell into a semi-depressed state. I felt sad, deflated and exhausted. My supervisor suggested I go to therapy. Rather than exploring my problem with alcohol—because I still did not believe it was a problem—I determined I wasn't challenged or stimulated, so I considered going to grad school yet again to get my PhD.

ENTERING THE MYSTICAL

I began searching higher education programs, but they all seemed like the same thing I had just finished. I was not feeling at all inspired. I started looking outside the traditional university path and discovered a utopia of alternative healing options. I had been exploring PhD programs in counseling and social work, and nothing had really sparked my interest. When I landed upon a program that listed courses such as dream interpretation, yoga, breath work, Reiki and chakra alignment, I was thrilled to be exploring new terrain.

I had felt spiritually dry since getting divorced. When I left the small town, I also left the church behind. My experience with church in the final days of the marriage had left me cynical about organized religion, and I hadn't set foot in a church since. I was frustrated with Christianity and how excluding it could be. I began questioning everything about it and often wondered if I was an atheist. However, I actually had a spiritual connection but didn't realize it. I felt very connected to nature and often found myself talking to the clouds and trees. At first, I didn't recognize what was happening. I was redefining my spirituality. I had also read *Conversations With God: An Uncommon Dialogue* by Neale Donald Walsch[1] and found his words very comforting. The book had given me hope that there might be another path.

---

[1] Walsch, Neale Donald. *Conversations with God: An Uncommon Dialogue.* New York: G.P. Putnam's Sons, 1996. Print.

I enrolled in the distance-learning program and began studying metaphysics. It was a term I had never heard before. But I liked the sound of it. I delved into courses on sacred topics and I couldn't get enough of it. As soon as I finished a course, I scoured the city looking for places where I could learn even more about the topic. My exploration didn't really feel like learning. The content was already inside of me, and I felt more as if it was finally activating. I felt a deep connection with holistic, natural healing. I can't describe it, but I felt it in my bones, my cells, even my hair follicles. I had never before felt as confident, competent or aligned with my life purpose as when I discovered these healing methods.

About the same time that I had lost faith in the church, I had also begun losing more and more faith in modern medicine. I had always believed in the healing power of the natural world, our bodies and the power of our thoughts. Even though society had never taught me to trust in these natural things, I inherently did. The metaphysics program affirmed my beliefs. I moved through the studies at a quick pace. I thoroughly trusted my intuition and knew I was on the right track. In my professional work, I began combining the healing therapies with traditional therapy, and the two paired well. I helped people tune into their own inner guidance mechanisms, their natural spiritual inclinations and the wisdom of their bodies. The combination helped clients discover the root of their issues rather than just mask or treat the symptoms. Once again, I was successful, which felt comfortable and familiar.

I was also using all of these practices in my own life and continuously learning, growing and trying to heal. At the time, though, I would not have described it as healing work on myself. I thought it was simply personal development. I didn't yet realize how sick I was. I had always suffered from anxiety and depression, but I wasn't aware of it because it was my "normal." And alcohol helped me manage both.

The non-profit agency that employed me was very supportive of my alternative healing approaches and allowed me to use many of my techniques in my work. They were also supportive in helping me move toward self-employment. They allowed me to work part time while I slowly built my own practice. I started the Holistic Growth Center and had the thrill of opening and growing my own business. Having never been one to shy away from a challenge, I jumped right in.

I was playing the roles of therapist, property manager, marketing rep, lawn keeper and janitor. The excitement of doing so many different things appealed to the part of me that needs constant stimulation. I never stopped to consider that opening a holistic center might be a rather impulsive thing to do for someone who had just discovered the holistic path a year before. Somehow, the business managed to be successful despite my naiveté.

My new adventures in holistic healing did not, however, keep me from drinking. Although, the new situation probably slowed my drinking, and it definitely made me more aware, it didn't stop me. I had become more aware because I was becoming more in tune with my body as well as my psyche. Subconsciously, I knew my constant preoccupation with alcohol couldn't be healthy. I had also thought that by moving onto what I perceived as a loftier career path the problem would somehow go away. All it did, however, was crank up the mental confusion, the emotional and spiritual confusion, and the confusion surrounding hypocrisy, as well. I was trying so hard to be a good person. I began viewing alcohol as a moral issue, and that activated my shame more than ever. Every time I drank too much, I felt as if I was not a good person. I carried around old programming that said drinking booze was bad in and of itself. Being drunk was really bad. Therefore, I was really bad, really often. I did not yet have the tools to look closely enough to consider that maybe it was just bad for me.

I was drinking less than I had in the past but experiencing stronger physical and emotional consequences. Alcohol is much harder on women than it is on men. We absorb and metabolize it differently. We have less tolerance, and the research is still out on exactly why. It could be hormones, stomach enzymes or less water in our bodies. Whatever the reason, it's twice as deadly for women as men. And I was experiencing how hard it is on the female body.

The fun of drinking began slipping away. Alcohol felt more and more like poison. My body wouldn't tolerate it anymore, and it often made me sick. I became less and less the fun-loving party girl. Alcohol no longer lightened me up; instead it weighed me down. Yet, I still psychologically craved it and craved how it used to make me feel. From the first sip, it had always been a reliable way to ease my anxiety and depression.

Now, it wasn't such a reliable friend. Sometimes it worked to loosen me up, but then the hangover the next day was more than just physical. The depression was overwhelming. Other times, the buzz never really kicked in, and alcohol took me deeper into depression right away. When I drank, I never really knew what to expect. But I couldn't imagine giving it up; sobriety as a way of life never even crossed my mind. I wished that I could somehow become a normal drinker. I wanted to be that person who is content with just one glass of wine. If I could have created my ideal drinking self, I would have been the person who never again drank so much that she had a hangover. I would simply drink in moderation, and it wouldn't be an issue. Much like coffee. I liked coffee. A lot! But I never had to worry about how much I consumed. I wasn't preoccupied with my coffee drinking.

FINDING A NEW DOCTOR

The Holistic Growth Center was comprised of two mental health counselors and a massage therapist. All three of us were energy healers, and we taught workshops. The city seemed ready for us and wanted what we had to offer. But I grew restless—as I tend to do.

I met an MD who was board certified in both allopathic and holistic medicine. I was quite taken with her. She was an intuitive, charismatic, beautiful Jamaican woman. She carried the wisdom and intrigue of her Jamaican heritage in stylish Madison Avenue clothing accessorized with lavish purses and shoes. She was a seductive blend, and she had star power. She wanted me to partner with her. I was like a middle-aged man snatching up a trophy wife. I abandoned the Holistic Growth Center and partnered with the doctor just two years after starting the business. Essentially, I walked out on my current partners and left them hanging.

The doctor and I complemented each other well, and I really enjoyed working with her. But at the same time, she really drew out my co-dependency. Before I knew it, I was more focused on wondering what would make her happy than truly following my intuition and being my authentic self. A big part of me believed I wasn't worthy of being her business partner, and I began to sabotage the situation by not being true to who I was or following my inner guidance. As in any relationship, when you stop being genuine, this shows through. I became far less appealing as a business partner. She was less attracted to my work because it was no longer authentic. I sensed her lessening attraction, and I struggled even harder to please her. There is nothing less attractive than someone fighting to be wanted. Our working relationship began to fall apart, and my income began to drop.

My anxiety built. But I didn't have the awareness to see what was going on within. I couldn't get in touch with what was brewing.

My body screamed to get my attention, too. I was very sick for an entire week. I experienced excruciating headaches, nausea, vomiting and a fever. The affliction would not let up, and I was admitted to the hospital with a diagnosis of spinal meningitis. I spent three days getting pumped with antibiotics. Being laid up gave me time to contemplate. I decided it was time for me to leave the partnership with the doctor. This was a typical pattern for me. I didn't know how to navigate discomfort or find meaning in it. My solution was always to leave. I bolted around our two-year mark. I did not realize that what I was running from was something within me, and it wasn't something I could ever escape. I had to come face to face with it.

I was incredibly confused. By all accounts, I had an amazing life. I had meaningful work and a longtime spouse whom I adored. I just couldn't identify what was wrong. Nothing felt right. I felt guilty and ungrateful. I constantly felt prickly and jumpy. My general reaction was to try to escape from everything. Fortunately, with all I had learned and was continuing to learn through my metaphysics program, I began to experience ways of slowing down. In the beginning, I never fully felt present when I did breath work, yoga or meditation. But these things had begun to help me become less hyper vigilant and anxious.

After leaving the doctor, I started working independently. Maybe I just wasn't cut out for having business partners. Maybe working solo was the answer. However, working alone led me to feeling isolated. I had been working on my own for about a year, and the phone calls and incoming clients began dwindling away. I was barely making any money. I no longer felt a sense of accomplishment. I had a lot of regret, thinking maybe I should have never left corporate. Or maybe I should have stayed at the non-profit agency where I was so fully supported. I was sure that I should have never abandoned my partners at the Holistic Growth Center, and I regretted leaving the doctor, too. I was filled with regret. And now I was alone with the exact same feelings I'd been trying to escape all along. I could run, but obviously I couldn't hide from what was going on inside. I could try and believe external circumstances were causing these feelings, but I was becoming suspicious that perhaps it was something living within me.

CRAZY AS A DAMN BAG OF SQUIRRELS

It was October. The weather was cooling off along with my incoming work. I had no new clients, and the repeat ones were canceling sessions. The rain poured for five days straight. The cloudy skies darkened my mood, and I wanted to crawl out of my skin. Like the weather, my anxiety would not let up. There was nothing specific troubling me. It was bigger than just work. I had begun to question everything I had ever known or believed. I wanted so desperately to escape my feelings, but I didn't have a clue as to how to go about doing so. I had never felt so out of control in my life. I felt shaky inside and out. I felt crazy. I wasn't sure what crazy was, but I had never felt the way I was feeling, and I was strongly suspicious that it was flat out craziness that I was experiencing. I was terrified to put voice to it and tell someone. I had never allowed myself to be vulnerable, and the thought of revealing to someone how I felt was terrifying. I was sure it would go away. But in those five days of rain, the intensity grew stronger and stronger.

Then an interesting thing happened at the end of the week. I discovered I had the keen gift of compartmentalizing the craziness. This was the week I had learned about my friend's suicide. Dennis was out of town. I updated him about the situation over the phone and told him I'd been feeling a "tad bit off." This was an understatement.

As the time approached for him to return home, I worked more diligently than ever to pull my stoic self together. I was afraid if I actually told someone (even him) how crazy I felt then it would make it so. I was determined to overcome the internal drama.

Having my man back in town reignited my co-dependent fire. I wanted to be the good wife and make sure that *he* was happy. My inner self believed I would not be loveable if I revealed how I was *really* feeling. A crazy wife does not make a good welcome-home present. And, we had to attend a work party for Dennis' company that night. So I did what any co-dependent, people-pleasing, low-maintenance wife would do. I pulled myself together. He needed a party girl bride, not a bat-shit crazy wife at his side.

I tucked away the craziness, even though it was barely suppressed under the surface. The party took place at the local VFW, which supplied me with plenty of cheap chardonnay, unlimited baskets of popcorn, a karaoke machine and adoring little old men. The chardonnay tamed the beast for a few hours.

It was a welcome reprieve from the anxiety and confusion. The next day I awoke to the familiar feeling of a dehydrated brain and queasy stomach. I was used to moving forward with a hangover. But on this particular day, I could barely get myself in the car and drive 45 minutes down the highway to the women's retreat I had signed up for. The retreat was about death and was taking place on Day of the Dead.

I was back to feeling crazy and once again ready to jump out of my skin. I felt as if every nerve in my body was on high alert. It was as if a cattle prod had taken a few good pokes at me. I felt shaky, nauseated and highly cautious. Of course, a night of drinking, ignoring my soul's troubles and hiding my feelings from my husband wasn't helping. I had sunk deeper into the abyss.

I went into the retreat. As the other women arrived, I just sat on the sofa and stared. I felt absolutely no desire to socialize, and wondrously, no one seemed to mind. I didn't bother to introduce myself to anyone. I was seriously clinging to my last shred of sanity. The crazy spell was reaching a tipping point. Something was about to give.

The guest facilitator from South America opened the retreat in her eloquent, exotic manner, and I worked hard to take what was coming out of her mouth and translate it into some form of meaning. Her words permeated my dehydrated brain cells.

Exotic Facilitator talked about how, for most of us, whatever our discomfort, in whatever emotional form it manifests, it ultimately comes down to a fear of death.

I suddenly discovered my voice, but it had no filters whatsoever. "I'm not afraid of death," I said.

I was a crazy woman on a mission to get my sanity back. I had been feeling this way for far too long now, and I wanted to get my act together. I wanted to feel sane and in control of my life.

"It's my plan B," I continued. "And I also need you to know I'm having a real crazy spell right now. I go from one extreme to another, from thinking I'm crazy as hell to considering I may be really enlightened. I just thought you should know that. Anyway, this whole death thing...I just keep going back and forth thinking things are really bad and then really good and then I'm so conf—"

"Drop into that," Exotic Facilitator said.

"What do you mean? Drop into it?"

"Drop into it."

"I don't understa—"

"Drop into it."

"But, I don't know what you m—"

"*Drop* into it."

"Drop into wha—" I was very irritated, and so tired.

"Deeper."

"But, what is d—"

"Deeper."

This woman would not let up.

"I...uh...ah..."

When I finally quit resisting her instructions, she softened a bit and guided me.

I dropped into a far deeper place within myself. I'd never been there before. It was quiet and dark, and that was okay. I had an image of butterfly wings taking shape. One side was black and the other white. The body of the butterfly formed. I saw it as my core. It's what holds the dichotomies together. I struggled to make sense of it. Perhaps it was showing me the dualistic thinking that lived deep within my cells. I believed that in order to be loveable I had to always be high functioning.

I have no idea how long I was in this surreal state. But a little bell rang and brought me out of the hypnotic trance. Exotic Facilitator then instructed us to go outside for the next hour. No talking. Just go and be at one with the land. She said she would ring the dinner bell when it was time for us to come in for lunch. And there would be no talking at that point either.

Exotic Facilitator annoyed me. She had sent me down a rabbit hole where I hadn't found any answers, and then she shooed me outside as if I were a child. I walked out into a bright, crisp October day. I was a little suspicious. The colors seemed a bit too vivid, too sharp. I was seriously suspicious that Exotic Facilitator somehow had the ability to alter my reality.

I knew she was expecting us to make our way around the 28 acres and be at one with the pond, the deer, the waterfall, but in my highly resistant, irritable state I walked only about three feet out the front door and plopped down spread-eagle underneath a tree.

I lay flat out on the ground. The resident German shepherd, Big, came to me and sat on my stomach. And, he continued to sit there for quite a while. It appeared that his intention was to hold me down. Even Big annoyed me. But, I finally gave up and let go. I attempted to drop back into wherever I had been before.

I closed my eyes and could see myself dropping through layers and layers. Dropping deeper, farther. Layers. Some were pitch black, some were vortexes. Layers and layers. Some were colors.

Dropping.

Dropping.

Sometimes I moved outward toward a deeper end, and other times it moved toward me. At one point, the void, the great silence, became extremely close. It got in my face. I felt nearly sick with claustrophobia. And, I knew I was getting close to the end of the mystical experience.

I slowed the process. I suddenly felt that I was very, very close to pure awareness. I panicked. What if I dropped into this full awareness? I knew it would isolate me from everyone. I already felt so different. I didn't need to isolate myself further. And, then I heard the voices of "everyone."

They were incredibly kind when they said that they were all already there and *they* had been waiting for *me*! It was a grand opportunity for embarrassment and shame, but instead I suddenly felt safer than I had in a while. I fully dropped in. I went there. I settled in to a place of stillness. It was not bliss, but it was also not uncomfortable. It just was. It was beyond space or time. It was the place that never goes away.

I suddenly knew that suicide would not make a bit of difference, because ultimately, I would never go away. It doesn't end. All the clichés about being more than just a body and being made of spirit suddenly made sense to me. Yes, I was a spiritual being having a physical experience. There was no beginning and no end.

I can't say that I was disappointed that it wasn't pure bliss. It felt realistic. I felt like I had answers. Then I heard the dinner bell. I sat up and opened my eyes and saw Exotic Facilitator motioning me back to the cabin. I felt as if I were moving through water.

We moved into the dining room and continued to observe the instructions of silence. I had never participated in a silent retreat, but I wasn't uncomfortable. Actually, I felt like talking might be difficult, so I welcomed the silence.

But, then my ego kicked in. Was I using the right fork? Was it okay to be eating my soup and salad simultaneously? Another woman had quickly finished all of her food. I sensed she was suddenly uncomfortable having done so, maybe even a little embarrassed. Exotic Facilitator nonchalantly enjoyed her meal, seemingly oblivious that the rest of us existed. My mind chatter revved up. I analyzed everyone else's actions. Not in a judgmental way, but with awareness. I began questioning if I was actually highly aware or if I was just absolutely fucking nuts. I waffled back and forth.

Another woman was trying to communicate by playing charades with hand gestures and facial contortions. She seemed to be trying to make people comfortable. That's when it hit me; I was seeing aspects of myself all around the table. I realized these women were all me. Every single person in the room demonstrated an aspect of me. Nothing existed that wasn't me. I had a deep sense of knowing that we were all one and the same. That we all shared many internal archetypes.

When this insight came, I was able to let go of any concerns about my performance. I felt so free. I could do anything I wanted. We finished our meals. Some women began clearing the table and going to the kitchen. But not me. I plopped down on the couch without feeling a single bit of guilt or obligation. I was simply being true to myself. I was emotionally exhausted, and I wanted only to sit. So rather than go through a mental conversation and overanalyze something as simple as whether or not to help with the dishes, I chose what I needed. And, it was okay.

Exotic Facilitator gathered us up after the meal and rang the little bell. Again, it was as if I had come out of a trance. I was no longer in an altered state, but the truth of what I had experienced did not change. And, I was able to look at Exotic Facilitator in a new way. I respected her, and I had connected with her. I left the retreat feeling different. Nothing was resolved but I knew I would never see the world the same again. I felt hope. I had been gifted with an up-close experience of the intelligence of the universe. I had dipped my toe into the mystical realms.

FASTER AND LOUDER

I continued to have insights and experiences like I did at this retreat, but I was the master at minimizing the experience and losing the learning very quickly. After getting a bit of space away from the experience, I would assume it wasn't nearly as powerful as I had originally thought. Or I would think I had just imagined it.

The one-day retreat had been very powerful and could have been viewed as a life changing experience, but, by the following week, I had let the experience go and resumed my struggle. I quickly returned to the same overwhelming anxiety with which I had entered the retreat. Rather than experience the powerful feelings, I fought hard to be relieved of my discomfort. I had always controlled most everything in my life and had the willpower and discipline to make whatever I wanted happen. However, these traits of diligence were only creating a deeper hole on this journey.

The end of October marked the 10-year anniversary of my departure from the corporate world to pursue a new and meaningful career. Yet, I felt like such a failure. I concluded that my entire professional life had been in vain. Every time I had been successful, I jumped ship. What was wrong with me? The mental chatter grew faster and louder. I couldn't sleep. It wouldn't turn off. I wasn't working, didn't have clients, and didn't have any ideas on what to do next. And I literally couldn't quit shaking. My body trembled. Finally, I went to see the doctor with whom I had been in partnership.

I went during lunch, knowing I would catch her without patients. She was in her office.

"Remember when we used to question how you know you're going crazy?" I asked her.

"Shut the door," she said.

I started crying and shaking even harder.

She asked a lot of questions from the standpoint of a friend.

"Are you and Dennis having problems?"

"No."

"Do you feel okay? Is the meningitis back?"

"No, I've really got something mental going on."

Then she asked questions from a clinical standpoint. And ended with asking if I had thought about hurting myself.

"No."

She finished by telling me I had to slow down my thoughts. She wrote out a prescription and handed me samples.

No! That's not what I wanted. But, I didn't have any other ideas, so I took the samples. Even before taking the medication I was starting to feel numb. Was this what it had come down to? I was a nutcase with a diagnosis and a prescription. A diagnosis of generalized anxiety hardly makes one a nutcase, but I knew intuitively that a prescription was not the answer I needed. Regardless, I filled the script.

Dennis was aware of my mental decline. But he was optimistic and kept expecting me to get better. For 15 years he had seen me accomplish whatever I had set my mind to. He was sure I would move through this, too. The medication numbed me, and I checked out. He was quiet. He couldn't fix it. He had kept making suggestions of things that typically helped me to feel better and was trying to will me back to sound health. He suggested more exercise. Or maybe longer meditations? How about sex? But it wasn't working. He felt helpless. I felt helpless and hopeless.

In my unbalanced mind, a prescription and diagnosis suggested I wasn't managing my life. I viewed the pills as a cop out, a quick fix. But, I had to admit, after just one pill, the thoughts were slowing down. I was very tired. I was sleepy. And, I was finally able to sleep.

I woke up about 2 a.m. feeling much different than I had in a while. I saw a veil. Yet another cliché. But in that moment I had a sudden realization. I knew I could continue on this path and keep taking medication to make my life feel more manageable and perhaps even find more meds to add to the cocktail. I could take this route and feel calm and numb. Or I could decide right then and there to take a different route. I knew there was a richness to be had by exploring this path of depression and anxiety. I wanted to take the dark excursion. I literally reached my hand out and broke through the illusory veil and suddenly everything was clear, sharp and vivid.

I was myself again. I was back in my own skin. I knew it wasn't fixed or finished. But I had hope that the experience was leading me to a better place. I had only taken that one dose of the medication. I threw the rest out. I made the decision to truly experience the journey, and I had the willingness to dig deeper along the way.

I felt a renewed hope about sanity, but I was not feeling any more confident about getting back on track with my professional work. I had lost all motivation for it. How could I possibly help others with their mental health when I barely had the energy to find my way out of the darkness? Yet my screaming mind continued to tell me I needed to work, make money, and be successful in order to matter. There was no part of me that was comfortable with just allowing myself to be still and immersed in the process. I had the absolute perfect scenario for being able to go deep and explore. I was self-employed. I had a break from clients. My husband made enough money to support us while I sorted things out. There is a lot of stigma associated with "breaking down," and I just couldn't fully surrender to taking a sabbatical. It felt like too huge of a step. There were too many parts of me that believed it was unacceptable to go to that dark place. The doctor had suggested that I just take some time off and figure my life out. But the voices screamed to get to work, stay busy, be productive, because these were the things that made me feel valued.

DESTROYING THE TAPES

No matter how hard I resisted it, I ended up with a sabbatical. There just was no work coming in. My schedule stayed absolutely empty. I didn't have the insight to just see it as a gift and embrace it. But I did take advantage of the opportunity to enjoy a weeklong stay at a beachfront resort in sunny San Diego at no cost. Two friends were going to a conference and had invited me to tag along. I was able to fly standby, and they were offering to share their room with me. Upon arrival we were upgraded to a studio apartment with a kitchen, living area, separate bedroom, and waterfront patio! I even had my own sleeper sofa.

I was supported in many ways during this soul-searching sabbatical. I spent my days walking. I could not quit walking. I would get up when the sun rose and walk until dark, up and down the beach. I'd try to sit and journal, but that wouldn't last long. I'd be back up walking. I walked the beach with no shoes. I walked the sidewalks with shoes. I wore out a pair of shoes. I had blisters on my feet. But I knew I had to walk. And I also went through the week without drinking, knowing that a clear mind was important. Going a week without drinking was highly unusual for me. I was willing to give it a try if it meant the return of my sanity.

My goal was to use the retreat to resolve my issues in one week's time. I intended to use every waking moment finding insight and every sleeping moment dreaming, processing and moving through my issues. I was certain that with enough diligence, I could be where I needed to be at the end of the seven days. But I was discovering hard work and determination weren't serving me as they always had in the past. There was that deep-seated belief that my worth came from how productive I was, how hard I worked. I found that I couldn't let go of the drive and simply experience what was happening. I really didn't know *how* to experience the moment. I was struggling hard to be out of the moment and back in to my comfort zone of being productive and successful. I had the willingness to not take a prescribed pill for the quick fix, but sadly I wanted my personal journey to only be a week long so that I could get back to the grindstone. My drive and tenacity, once great characteristics, were now biting me in the ass.

Through the walking, I found a bit of clarity and did feel some sense of peace. I was able to recognize how I was being provided for in huge ways with the flight, the pullout couch and friends who were allowing me to crash with them. I felt gratitude. Real gratitude. I realized I had always intellectualized what I was grateful for, but hadn't actually felt it deep within my cells. I felt gratitude for the sound of the ocean and the colors in the sunset. I watched with pure fascination how quickly the sun sank behind the horizon. My normal gratitude list included my health, my husband, a nice home and a supportive family. I would go through and analyze the things in my life that people in third-world countries didn't have and then experience a blend of guilt and gratitude. But when I listed these things in my mind, I was actually making more of a plea that these things not go away rather than feeling gratitude deep within. This sudden new feeling of gratitude was powerful. I was actually *experiencing* gratitude. I felt it rather than just thought about it. The energy radiated out from my heart center.

During this searching period, I found it hard to determine if I was actually following my inner guidance or acting out of fear because I felt desperate in so many ways. I had always lived a life of fearlessly following my inner voice. This is how I was able to leave my dead-end first marriage and the corporate life. I knew my soul longed for more and went after it even though doing so wasn't easy. I was willing to follow my soul instead of logic. Now, I couldn't discern the truth in my inner voice. I tried feeling it in my body, but that seemed to be inconsistent, too. All former systems of knowing were breaking down within me. No longer trusting myself was overwhelming.

While in San Diego, I dreamed about boxes of old cassettes. In the dream I was giving some of them away but holding onto some of the old ones I really liked. The meaning was obvious. How was I going to give up what I was still holding on to? And even more important, how was I going to discern *what* old tapes I was struggling to let go of.

This was about my beliefs that weren't working any more. I had always believed that I could only be valued or loveable if I was productive, hard working and thin. I also often believed that no one really wanted to hear what I had to say, so it was best to just be quiet. There were more subtle beliefs, too, such as, *I'm not a good person if I get angry.* These beliefs had been ingrained since birth and had even been passed down from previous generations. They were all I'd ever known, and they'd worked to some degree over the years.

A HOMER SIMPSON MOMENT

When I returned from the San Diego getaway, it was time for a follow-up visit with the doctor/friend. She was pleased to hear that I had made sense out of a lot of things and had decided to take the route of sanity. We discussed the insights I had gained. The visit was about up, and I heard my voice saying, "but I really need to do something about this drinking."

Oops, did I say it out loud?

Yes, it was out loud. I don't know why I was concerned. My doctor friend knew about my drinking habits. We had often talked about my concerns, usually over drinks. This time, though, we were discussing my concerns in a clinical setting rather than at a friendly happy hour.

She first responded with physician protocol and asked specifically how much I drank, if anyone had told me I had a problem with alcohol, or if I'd gotten a DUI or anything similar. No, none of these things were the real problem. And she knew this.

"Okay," she said. "Doctor hat off; friend hat on." She asked me a very important question. "Do you *feel* in your heart that drinking is a problem for you?"

Ow! Why couldn't she have asked what I thought, what my head tells me, or even what the assessments tell me?

"Yes," I said. "I know it's a problem."

The topic of self-medicating and trying to numb out feelings came up, and I quickly said, "I know, but I can't figure out what it is that I'm trying to escape."

"If you stop drinking, you'll figure out what you're numbing." *Ouch.* Such a simple statement of common sense. Yet so harsh.

Doh!

I let her know I wasn't ready. I had enough to deal with, and giving up my coping strategy didn't sound very appealing. I left quickly, but, as soon as I got in the car, I realized I *had* to do it. I realized it had been hanging over my head for what seemed like forever. So, I thought about what it would be like to go home and enter the evening without a glass of wine or a few sips of icy vodka. What would I do, what would I think, what would I feel? I imagined freeing a dark monster. But instead of fear, I felt relief.

Relief? What a welcome change.

I realized that I had been smart enough to manage my drinking so that it never became an issue for anyone but me. No one had ever told me my drinking was a problem. I wasn't mean. I didn't drink and drive. So, what was the problem if I had all these areas mastered? The problem was that I personally was not at peace with how much alcohol consumed my thoughts. I had a drink or two or three every night, sometimes more. It was a toxic pattern for me. There was a strong emotional dependence. When I examined my drinking habits, I realized I used all occasions as an excuse to drink. I drank to unwind from a stressful day, to gear up for a social setting, as a reward for whatever. The list goes on. When I wasn't drinking, I thought about when I would drink next. If I was in a drinking setting, I scanned the room to see how much others were drinking. I checked out how much alcohol was available and devised a strategy for keeping my glass full without arousing suspicion.

The sense of relief I felt at the thought of quitting was a red flag. I had a real problem. But that realization didn't stop the rationalizing and analyzing from kicking in. I had the brief thought of cutting back, but I didn't really bother to go there. I had spent 15 years working at cutting back, and it hadn't worked. Sure, I was a much more responsible drinker than I had been 10 years prior. But now the alcohol was eating away at my soul.

And my body had become less and less tolerant of the toxin. I had chronic sinus issues, constipation and digestive issues to the point that I had rectal bleeding, and it definitely seemed irritated by drinking. It had started slowly and infrequently, but it was still a bit alarming to have blood coming from my rear. Eventually it became more frequent, and I never knew when it would happen. It often happened at the most inopportune times. I once bled through my clothes onto someone's nice chair. And another time I was at a social function and suddenly noticed blood running down my leg. Yes, it was incredibly humiliating, especially knowing that the condition was most likely alcohol related. My hope was that people would simply think I was having a really rough menstrual cycle. I would have been horrified if anyone knew I was gushing blood from my ass because I couldn't lay off of the chardonnay.

When I went to the gastrointestinal specialist about the digestive issues, I was honest on the paperwork about how much I drank. The doctor didn't mention it or suggest that I quit. Subconsciously, I was asking for medical intervention. When I did my own research, I discovered that alcohol has a horrible effect on the gastrointestinal system. Having this much knowledge was taking the fun out of drinking.

Sometimes I would have one drink and be totally incapacitated, and other times I could have five drinks and not feel a thing. Hangovers were horrendous. My body was fighting the poison. Drinking did not resonate with the rest of my life. I was seeking a spiritual path that demanded clarity and a willingness to fully experience life. The path I had undertaken required that I fully experience my emotions and bring awareness to all aspects of the journey.

Alcohol knocked me out of balance. My preoccupation with drinking took up psychic space, and the actual act of drinking fogged any hope of crystal clear perception. I had never been totally clear, conscious and aware. I had been numbing or comforting myself with substances since I was a child. I didn't have an understanding of what my soul was asking for because I had never experienced it. And I had no idea how blissful consciousness could actually be. Perhaps if someone had told me that conscious sobriety and recovery was a beautiful process, I might have sought it sooner and more willingly.

I called a friend that I frequently made self-deprecating jokes to and told her that I was in the midst of making up my mind to quit. She liked to drink, too. When I told her my decision, she tuned in as if I had said I had found the fountain of youth. "We have to talk," she said. "I want in."

Huh? She wanted in? We met and hiked, and she admitted that her drinking habits were something she was very concerned about, too. She wanted to stop, and she wanted to have a partner to ease the burden. This was becoming easier than I expected.

I started discussing whether or not we should attend recovery meetings together, even though this was one area that I vehemently resisted. I knew the stereotypes of being one of "those people." I had no interest in the smoky basements of block buildings where the dregs of society slugged coffee and told their secrets in raspy, nicotine voices. But for the first time, I thought maybe the fact that I was so resistant was a sign that I needed what they had to offer. My friend was even more opposed to meetings than I was. She was even open to a temporary pause rather than totally quitting. This started to scare me, but it also challenged me. I saw myself in her resistance, and it motivated me to say, "No. I am quitting!"

CAN'T LIVE WITH YOU
CAN'T LIVE WITHOUT YOU

Finally a few days later I did it. I quit drinking. I didn't have a plan. I just woke up and decided I was no longer drinking. As I expected, it was a relief and I felt lighter. I stayed on my pink cloud of sobriety for several weeks and proudly announced to family and friends that I was no longer a drinker. I didn't go to recovery meetings or have a plan in place. I just stopped drinking and resumed the rest of my life. But then something snuck up on me. I started feeling like…okay I'm sober, is this it? Now what? Is this all there is? I felt a vacancy inside. I felt a void.

I quit drinking and assumed that my reward would be that everything else would fall into place. My underlying belief was that drinking was a moral issue, and if I took the high road then I would be rewarded with success and financial gain. It wasn't happening. So, I had a glass of wine. That didn't work either. I didn't enjoy it. I was so confused. I was trying so hard, yet nothing seemed to be working. So I squirmed back into the familiarity of my normal way of drinking, welcoming wine and vodka back as my nightly companions. I wasn't happy with them, and I was miserable without them.

During this period of sobriety, I had a meditation in which I met my future self. The ultimate all-the-way-out-there future self. She was beautiful. She had long, flowing red hair. She was graceful. She wore blue-green mermaid colors, and she shimmered. Her name was Calista. Calista may have looked all flowy and goddess-like, but she had attitude. I liked her. She was accessible. I closed my eyes and she was there, full of wisdom and guidance. She was incredibly sensual and confident. She danced all the time. She was so light. She kept reminding me that she is me. At one point I burst into tears, realizing this was how beautiful I am, but then the realization was gone.

Calista wanted me to focus on my passion. She told me my life would flow when I fully committed to the path, committed to my purpose and made it a priority. If I did that, I would see how everything lined up and flowed. She also told me there were many books already written within me. When I write, I will gain clarity. She kept telling me to focus and commit. I had a few meditations where she showed up. And then one day, for no apparent reason I couldn't tap into her energy. Calista was no longer accessible. Did she get tired of me ignoring her wisdom? Or was I just scared of her? Probably both.

MOXIE ANGELS

During this period of self-exploration and growing frustration, I continued to feel like I couldn't win. My work appeared to have been taken away from me, so I tried my best to finally surrender. I made an effort to view the lack of work as an opportunity to focus on my own healing. I was still resistant, but I was trying. And then, while I was in a freaking yoga class for God's sake, my Jeep was stolen.

I was so discouraged. I had hidden my keys in the toe of my shoe. I tried hard to find the gift in the situation, but the vehicle was an older model, and I only had collision insurance. *Poof!* It was gone. The police had no leads whatsoever. I tried to make sense of it. Perhaps the incident was symbolic of how my drive had disappeared. Ultimately, the only lesson I gleaned from the situation was to not hide my keys in the toe of my shoe.

I quit drinking a second time.

And for the second time I started right back.

The problem was that after several weeks of clarity and sobriety, I could convince myself I didn't really have a problem. I could handle drinking in a responsible way. And I was certain that I would never go back to my old habits.

Just one glass certainly wasn't going to hurt anything. Right?

I would enjoy it and be done. But that one sip would set off another chain of events. I would obsess about my next *just one glass.* My thoughts were once again consumed with when I could enjoy my next drink or two.

In hindsight, this is very telling. Most alcoholics spend a lot of time and energy trying to prove we can drink like other people. It becomes an obsession to somehow become a normal drinker. For some, it's a lifelong obsession that eventually kills them.

I quit drinking yet *again*.

I had been sober for several weeks and was thriving in my newfound state. Then came Monday Night Football. To make matters more intense, this was the biggest game of the year for us because the Titans rarely got to play on Monday night. Football was one of the interests that Dennis and I passionately shared. I particularly liked tailgating and the unapologetic consumption of alcohol that occurred at games. I decided I was doing so well, that drinking in celebration of this "monumental" event only made sense. I arrived at the stadium feeling fabulous and somewhat excited that I had a free pass to drink. I had my first drink. Then I tossed back another.

Those two drinks not only stole my clarity and peace, they hit me hard. I became stumbling drunk. No build up. No entertaining, fun part. I went straight from tranquil to apathetic and drunk.

I had taken the following day off and I awoke feeling sluggish and toxic. I didn't have a hangover, but I had put enough alcohol into my body to disturb it. My thoughts raced all day. The underlying anxiety, depression and self-deprecation came back with a vengeance.

I was so very, very tired of this pattern. I had been on this soul-searching journey for one year, and it seemed as if I'd made no progress. I was used to getting things done, but this time I felt stuck.

I sat on the deck of our little lake cabin, surrounded by a collage of autumn colors. The sky was a brilliant blue. It was the most perfect day, but I was depressed. I tried to journal away my woes, but everything I wrote was so cyclical, the rehashing of the same issues over and over. I looked out at the crisp and colorful view; it was bright, vivid and alive. I listened to the rhythm of the birds chirping and the water slapping against the bank. I inhaled the very distinct fragrance of life on Tennessee water, a mossy blend of pine and cedar. I knew this collaborative effort that Mother Nature had put on display for me was really my true self. This was who I was. I was an earthy, colorful goddess… Yes, a goddess. Not polluted, heavy and dark. I frantically tried to write my way to a solution. Then I heard an inner voice.

"Get off your fat ass and quit being a victim."

In that moment, I knew I had just reached another turning point. I took this rallying call seriously. I *was* being a victim, and I couldn't keep doing the same thing and expecting a different result.

I've always known I have dark humor angels surrounding me. I believe I have divine guidance around me all the time, but it never feels like fluffy white wings, harps or cherubic faces. My angels have moxie. They have edges and attitudes. And on this particular day, they were bored with my recurring story. I could almost see them rolling their eyes at my accusations that alcohol had stolen my clarity.

No, I had done this to myself.

Why do I keep acting like such a victim?

I allowed it. Invited it. Alcohol was my abusive boyfriend. I had found a new life that met all of my needs, yet I didn't believe there was any way I could be happy on my own. I always went running back to alcohol, begging for another chance. My peace had not been stolen. I had handed it over freely. I had stood there—arms wide open—and begged alcohol to please come back to me.

Here I am. I am offering up my clear brain to you to become fuzzy and dehydrated. Please enter my entire system so that I can feel shaky and uncertain. Tie up my emotions and make me question everything. Insert yourself as a heavy dark fog between me and my higher self. Yes, do all of these things…hurry!

TUNE IN AND LISTEN

Time to detox. First step, a cleanse. I went on a three-day juice fast and really felt a shift in the recurring pattern. I believed I was able to finally do something different. After the three-day fast, I added organic fruits and vegetables to my diet, but I wasn't sure what the new normal was going to be.

Then a book serendipitously landed in my path and introduced me to the merits of a vegan lifestyle. Once I had read about factory farming and the torture that animals endure, I knew I would never be able to look at meat the same way again. Dairy also had its problems. I read everything about plant-based diets I could get my hands on. The change in diet was key for me. Eating whole foods that were alive and colorful felt healing. My body felt strong and clear. I had no desire to pour alcohol into it. Colors seemed brighter, and my mind felt at peace. I rarely had racing thoughts. I felt a new lightness I hadn't experienced with all of my other ventures into sobriety.

I remained sober for a few weeks.

Then a month.

Two months. Three months.

The rectal bleeding went away. I felt absolutely amazing.

Life became much easier. Everything flowed, and I was no longer afraid.

I fell in love with sobriety. Several people offered to take me to recovery meetings, but I really didn't see the point. I wasn't struggling. The change in diet seemed to have made a huge difference. I was certain I had found the key this time. I felt virtuous and clean from the inside out. I knew I was on the right path.

SAND DOLLARS

My professional life once again began to take shape. I planned a seven-day women's retreat in Southern California. I had organized this type of event before and I was fully enjoying utilizing the skills it took to plan, market and facilitate. I put the info about the retreat out into the world, and women registered. This was a wonderful feeling.

I was excited to facilitate a retreat and not feel like a hypocrite for the first time. I was no longer drinking, so I believed that by having a bit of sober time under my belt and no intentions to drink again I had recovered. That I was done. Fixed. Healed. I had finally arrived in that successful professional state I had been craving for so long.

Courtney, my hairdresser, was participating in the retreat. She was 26 years old, three years sober and very active in a recovery program. She kept inviting me to meetings with her.

I assumed my sobriety was very different than hers. I had had a spiritual practice in place *before* I got sober, so I felt I was somewhat unique in my path. And the clean, plant-based diet was an added benefit. I didn't want to go to recovery meetings. I considered myself very different than people who went to meetings, and I felt confident I had finally conquered my demon.

Courtney asked if the retreat schedule would allow her time to take in a couple of meetings during the week. I assured her I would get her to a meeting.

"You could go with me," she said.

I declined.

On the night before the retreat I had just celebrated four months of sobriety, my longest stint yet. My retreat materials were packed. I was eagerly anticipating the upcoming seven days away and my early morning flight, when all of a sudden I thought about the bottle of vodka in the basement freezer. Since I was going to be on retreat for a week, there was no way I could drop back into a pattern, so it somehow made sense to just have a small drink to celebrate.

Celebrate sobriety with a drink?

Yes, that's how the alcoholic mind works.

I drank a tiny bit of vodka. It slid down my throat with ease; it warmed my stomach. I sat and stared out of my living room window. I kept refilling the glass with just a half shot. I was in somewhat of a trance. It felt like pure bliss to have my comfort back. Yet, simultaneously, I was disgusted with myself. I then went out to dinner and I had two drinks with my virtuous plant-based meal. Then I came home and finished off the bottle of vodka. I had already broken my four-month cycle of abstinence, so it only made sense to consume as much as I possibly could. I couldn't stop until the bottle was gone. And when it was gone, I was horrified. It was as if something had taken over my mind and body.

I awoke the next day feeling lower than I'd ever felt in my life. I was shocked. I was so disappointed in myself. The depression that followed was excruciating. I headed off to California with the deepest sense of humiliation and disgrace. I wanted to cancel the trip because I felt I was in no way capable of leading others on a retreat. I was a mess. I went, but I was terrified and wracked with shame. I had been fooling myself for four months.

It was the scariest point in my life. I felt doomed and I didn't know where to turn. It never entered my mind that a rehab program might be an option. It never entered my mind to ask for help.

I didn't tell anyone on the retreat what I'd done. I walked around with my dark secret tucked away, breeding more shame in my already shame-filled soul. And as a visual reminder, the rectal bleeding returned.

I had to face the fact that I couldn't trust myself. I felt hopeless. I was facilitating a women's holistic retreat, and yet I still had a very big problem that I thought I had solved. I felt like such an imposter. As the week went on, thankfully the depression lifted, but I recognized that I was facing an ongoing battle. I realized if I didn't do something drastic, alcohol would kill me. Either the alcohol itself would put me under or the extreme depression that followed drinking would do me in.

Two nights before our retreat ended, one of the participants told the story of her mother's battle with alcoholism. Her mother was going to outpatient treatment and also struggling with depression. This daughter, on a chilly day, had gone to pick her mother up to take her to a therapy appointment. The mother said, "Let me get my sweater," and went to the basement. The daughter heard the gun shot and rushed down the stairs to find her mother dead.

As I listened to this excruciating story, I imagined myself descending the steps and never returning. I knew without a doubt that something had to give. Hearing this story was a gift, another wake up call. I really was at my bottom. I could not live this way any longer. I had tried over and over to manage this on my own. It was not working.

The next day I spent the afternoon walking on the beach contemplating my dire situation. I asked the universe for help. I acknowledged that I could not think my way out of this life-threatening situation. I admitted I did not have the answers. I begged for guidance.

I kept finding sand dollars. Whole sand dollars. I had a stack of them. I thought it must be sand dollar season.

When I got in for the evening, I discovered that no one else had found *any* sand dollars. I shared my riches with everyone. Suddenly, I felt like the sand dollar symbolized a recovery chip.

I looked at Courtney. I felt such gratitude and respect for her and all that she had accomplished. She had done something—that with all my diligence, intellect, and perceived self-awareness—I couldn't do. I was humbled.

"If I were to decide to try a recovery program, could you be my sponsor?" I asked.

"Yes I can," she said. "Would you like for me to?"

And that was the moment I finally surrendered. I knew I was no longer on this journey alone. I was ready to acknowledge and receive a power greater than myself. I was no longer in charge.

This moment was especially humbling for me because I was the leader of the retreat and had allowed myself to be as vulnerable as I'd ever been in my life. I risked having all the participants see me as a drunk and demand their money back, or to publicly ridicule me and have my professional name smeared for life. It wasn't an experience that I had the opportunity to think through. When a moment of grace comes, it's not a thinking thing. It's simply a divine moment, and that's what I experienced.

If I had been given the time to think it through, I'm sure I would not have allowed myself to show such vulnerability. While it was not the most professional thing I could have done, I have absolutely no regrets and no doubt this divine moment saved my life.

I had always been resistant to recovery programs. I had attended a few during the grad school addictions class. They had felt so depressing. I remember an atmosphere of fear and desperation. Of course, at the time, I was looking for every way possible to separate myself from the people in the meetings. But this time, I had to let go of my judgment about the program. It had a long history of success, and I didn't.

PSYCHIC CHANGE

Courtney gave me the recovery text from the program, and I began reading it on the flight home. I willed myself to remain open as I read. I didn't want my intellectual mind to control the process. I learned many things. The author explained that alcoholics were essentially allergic to alcohol. The average temperate drinker does not experience the same type of cravings that the alcoholic experiences. And unless the alcoholic can experience an entire psychic change, there is little hope for him or her to recover.

The author's story hit me hard. He wrote about how on the morning after a drunk fest his brain raced uncontrollably with remorse, horror and hopelessness.

I was shocked by the similarities between what he had experienced in 1929 and what I was experiencing almost a century later. He wrote that he had continued drinking for two more years and feared for his sanity.

Uh yeah, this man and I have a definite connection.

And then he finally surrendered. Once he truly let go, he was catapulted into what he called the "fourth dimension of existence," where he came to know happiness, peace and usefulness.

My heart raced, and I was near tears as I read this. *Yes, Yes, Yes!* This is what I wanted, and I believed I could have it, too. I suddenly had an entirely new view of the recovery program. The founder had clearly experienced a mystical transformation. And I could, too.

Actually, I already had. Those sand dollars and Courtney's presence were no coincidence. That was divine intervention. The book said that you have to be willing to believe in a power greater than yourself.

I did.

The steps of the program were suddenly making a lot more sense than they had in the past. I had always been especially resistant to Step One: admitting I was powerless.

Step One – We admitted we were powerless over alcohol – that our lives have become unmanageable.

These simple words had a totally different meaning than they ever had in the past. Now I saw I really was powerless over alcohol. I had never liked the word "powerless" and didn't like the idea of labeling myself as an alcoholic and saying I was powerless. But after my experience with the sand dollars and with Courtney, I finally understood what it was about.

I am and will always be powerless over alcohol. Once I take the first sip, then I give all my power away. At that point, alcohol controls me. And the scary part is that I never know how it will turn out. For example, during the Monday Night Football scenario, I only had two drinks. I was able to quit after that. That incident left me feeling is if I were in control of my drinking. It gave me a false sense of control. But on the eve of the retreat, I had zero control. I didn't plan to drink like that. I was powerless once I took the bottle of vodka out of the freezer and took the first sip.

I would always be powerless over alcohol. My life didn't appear unmanageable to the outside world, but my inner emotional state was a train wreck. I couldn't stay in the crazy-making state I had been in for the past year. So at this point, I could also concede that, yes, my life had become unmanageable.

For the first time in my adventures in sobriety, I realized I could never ever drink again. That was the barrier that had held me back before. I had never fully surrendered the drinking. *Normal drinking* was always looming out there as a possibility. I felt a huge sense of relief when I finally made the commitment to never drink again.

Going the recovery program route was serious business. When I had quit drinking before, I had taken a lighthearted approach. I viewed it as something similar to cleaning up my diet. I had lumped it in with giving up dairy and meat. In my mind, giving up alcohol was just a cleaner way of living. This approach only served to insulate me from the true problem of alcoholism. This wasn't just a dietary issue. Alcoholism is a disease, a disease that has no cure. Fortunately, it does have a solution, and I had finally found it.

I am an alcoholic.

I had to admit this to myself. I was no longer just a party girl who couldn't get her problem drinking under control.

Admitting it to others was a big deal, too. When you enter a recovery program, people look at you differently. Saying the word "alcoholic" makes people uncomfortable. I knew that if I exposed myself to the world in this capacity, I could never go back to drinking. I had far too much pride. Yes, this was a serious commitment.

MY TERMINAL UNIQUENESS

I got home from the retreat and began going to recovery meetings. Unfortunately, the meetings were as I remembered. They were not as encouraging as reading the book on the plane had been. There were a lot of really sad people. There were people who were continuously relapsing and drinking unbelievably huge amounts of alcohol. There were people who were going to meetings every single day just to stay sober. Oh, God, it was depressing.

I told Courtney I wasn't like them.

She said, "Not yet!"

Okay, okay. I had agreed to do it her way, and she was cutting me no slack. I kept going. I tried out different meetings and I even bought a journal to take with me. I doodled and jotted down things I heard that were helpful. I let go of the things that weren't.

I had been going to meetings for almost a month and still hadn't said the dreaded words: "Hi, I'm Tammy and I'm an alcoholic."

This was mainly because I didn't have anything to say. I was there to listen at this point, but I definitely dreaded saying *the* word. I was a month into my recovery program when I wrote in my journal:

> *I struggle with what to make of the program stuff. I don't like it. But, I'm scared to go without it.*

I kept going. Sobriety felt different. When I had taken a sabbatical from drinking previously, I had always lived with the hope that I would return to drinking in a normal way. This time it was permanent, and I had to discover a new way to live.

I was showing up at social functions fully awake, aware and sober. I attended family gatherings without my buffer. I had to go to functions where others were drinking and I wasn't. Often, I felt like a raw nerve suddenly exposed to cold air.

I had to find a new social life. I didn't want to just continue the same life without alcohol. I wanted to create a new vibrant life. I knew I could keep going to sporting events, concerts and parties and simply enjoy a glass of bubbly water instead, but that wasn't what I wanted. I wanted something fresh.

I had periods of apathy. I didn't know what to do with my time. Living without alcohol felt like dry toast. *What's the point?* I also felt resentful that I couldn't drink like other people. And, I felt a lot of fear. I didn't know how to live this way.

When the difficult emotions were there, I had to learn to fully experience them rather than find another way to numb them out. It was time to truly change my life. Fortunately, most of the time I actually felt clear, energized and optimistic. But fear lurked in the shadows.

My sobriety also brought many amazing dreams. Two of these were especially inspiring. First, I dreamed I had won 100-million dollars and realized I could do anything I wanted. The dream suggested I needed to think bigger. I awoke from the second dream with a very specific sentence echoing in my thoughts: "The universe gives in very generous ways." These two dreams led me to believe that I needed to open up and allow myself to surrender to my full potential. I felt a little overwhelmed, but mainly I was really excited. *How does one surrender to her full potential?* The short answer is to listen and follow your intuition in every moment. But actually doing that is a daunting task. I suppose it's something I will attempt to master for the rest of my life.

WORKING THE STEPS

As part of my recovery process, Courtney asked me to write out every single thing I could think of that I regretted doing while I had been drinking. I had to list every embarrassing memory.

Ouch.

Listing all of the shameful occurrences was overwhelming.

Is this really such a great idea?

I followed Courtney's advice. She said I could return to the list if I ever thought about touching alcohol again. I knew it would be very hard to take a sip with all of those memories swirling around.

I read everything I could get my hands on related to recovery. I read *A Woman's Way through the Twelve Steps*, by Stephanie Covingiton[2]. I found that women-only meetings were the best fit for me. The women in these meetings seemed to share a common thread of shame and guilt. I definitely had moments when I got caught up in a shame spiral. Thankfully, many women who had long-term sobriety also showed up. They filled the space with hope and strength.

I was working the steps and allowing deep-seated issues to rise to the surface. As a chronic overachiever, I wanted to get all of the recovery done and be recovered. But that's not

---

[2] Covington, Stephanie. *A Woman's Way through the Twelve Steps*. Center City, MN: Hazelden, 1994. Print.

how it works. There was only one way, and that was to go directly through. I had to feel, experience and endure it all. And I now know that it never ends. It's a lifelong process. Layer after layer. But at least I'm learning to appreciate the process and not view it as so daunting. Every time I get through another layer of healing, insight and meaning, I feel lighter and brighter.

I felt more at ease at the meetings. I began speaking. I finally stepped up and said the dreaded words: "My name is Tammy, and I am an alcoholic."

It wasn't so bad.

I reached three months of sobriety...of recovering sobriety. It was different from the three-month marks I had reached in the past. I was dealing with life fully sober. The good and the bad.

With each new sober day, I continued to feel more and more emotions. I had spent a lifetime numbing out the bad feelings. Sobriety made me realize I had also been numbing out the joy. Now my highs were incredibly high. I would sometimes become overwhelmed with happiness. I felt like a toddler taking my first few steps; suddenly I was off and running. Sometimes I would fall down, but soon I'd pop back up again. Everything felt new.

I discovered new ways to spend my time. I've always been a lover of books and reading, but during my drinking days, I would only read for a short while until the buzz kicked in and all focus disappeared. Now, I actually spent entire evenings reading and finishing books. I found that my friendships changed. I preferred spending time with people I could have authentic, deep conversations with, rather than those who only liked to get together for frivolous chatter. In the past, we had done that over drinks.

I quit attending things that I connected with alcohol. Initially, I gave up work parties and gatherings that had open bars. I quit going to NFL games. Yes, I loved football, but I had also loved the tailgating and daylong drinking that went along with it. I started going to yoga on Sunday mornings rather than downing Bloody Marys.

I attended kirtan (a musical form of yoga) on Saturday nights and discovered this brought on an entirely different kind of buzz, with no hangover. I joined an artist co-op that was based on exploring creativity rather than just creating art. There was no pressure, just creative expression. I set up a little space at home where I could meditate, journal or do artwork. Having my own space was a great reminder of the importance of self-care.

Self-care was not something I had learned growing up, or in college or in the workplace. The counseling field talked about it for clients, but I had never mastered it. I also started really enjoying being home and catching up on movies, books, and doing a lot of self-help, recovery-based work. I attended meetings and met people for coffee. I went to bed early and got up early on the weekends and went for long hikes. I attended group meditations and other spiritual gatherings. I sought out new forms of peace. I was a bit shocked in the beginning to discover that there was this entire world of happenings on Saturday nights that didn't include alcohol.

Who knew?

In the throes of my drinking, I had had a spiritual practice (meditating, yoga, etc). In recovery, I learned that this is called having a spiritual bypass. I had tried with all of my might to use my spiritual journey to avoid doing the real work. There were no bypasses happening now. This journey was the real deal.

HAPPY, JOYOUS AND FREE

My career continued to grow. I began offering more and more holistic workshops for women in which I taught them how to follow their inner guidance. It has been said that you teach what you need to learn. I also applied for several counseling jobs. I followed where my energy guided me rather than trying to make something happen for the sake of my ego. This was progress.

I started a holistic facilitators training program and began training others to facilitate workshops and retreats. It was a very experiential process. We were doing deep personal work, and it challenged me to bring every bit of my authentic self into play. It also challenged me to fully trust myself. Sobriety was building my self-worth. I had always had self-confidence and believed I could do whatever I set my mind to, but now I was finally seeing myself as worthy and good.

I reached the six-months sober mark and continued to feel happy, joyous and free, just as the recovery program had promised me. Unfortunately, it was about this time that the holistic facilitators' group had an eruption. The group split, and three of the members dropped out. They blamed me for all that had gone wrong. However, this proved a great opportunity for me to really practice mindfulness. So much of my self-esteem had been wrapped up in what others thought of me professionally. The three individuals who had dropped out were not at all happy with me. They sent letters and emails with scathing accusations of how I had let them down. I could have easily gotten lost in a shit storm of shame and agreed with every disparaging word about my incompetence. But I didn't. Instead, after a lot of meditating, self-talk, and processing with others, I took a look at the facts.

I recognized I could have done plenty of things differently with the training. I hadn't done anything illegal, immoral or unethical, but I hadn't facilitated or communicated as well as I could have, either. I wasn't a bad person. I just hadn't done a very good job. I would do better next time. I owned my part of the wreckage, but I wasn't going to own it all and fall on my sword. I hoped that others would own their emotions, and I let it go. Now that's not to say that I didn't find myself occasionally obsessing and worrying about it, but I vowed to shift my old pattern. I gave myself permission to screw up professionally. Of course, admitting I hadn't done a good job was difficult.

The four who remained in the group showed me compassion, and I practiced having some for myself. This was new. Having unrealistic, perfectionistic standards for myself had never really served me well. Changing this pattern was important.

TRUSTING MY GUT

I had a lot of work to do to rebuild my professional confidence. I was still a bit wobbly in the knees. I needed something to help me fully own my strengths and rid me of my fears.

Ask and ye shall receive.

The non-profit agency I had left six years prior recruited me to work in a crisis shelter for teens. It felt good to be wanted. I wasn't especially excited about the job, but it felt right. I kept wondering why I was there, but I sensed there was a purpose behind it all. I tried not to question the gift. It was a means to get back on my feet emotionally, professionally and financially.

Logically, this position was a step backwards in my career. I was hesitant to leave the path of facilitating retreats, workshops, writing and such. But intuitively, this felt very much like the right step. The director wanted to integrate holistic programming. She was open to me adding yoga, meditation and other mindfulness activities. I accepted the position.

Then, on my first day, the director resigned. When I heard the news, my first thought (after a tad bit of feeling abandoned), was that I should take her place. But my gut told me not to act on that urge. I was very good at acting impulsively. This time, I looked but I didn't leap. I was really tuning into my intuition and higher power.

Over the next few weeks, I continued to think about applying for the director position, but I also felt it wasn't the right time. I waited two months. The shelter did not fill the role. Suddenly, I felt the time was right. Yet, I still did not leap.

First, I created a list of pros and cons. All logic said to run fast from this job. It was a 24-7-365-days-a-year operation that dealt with some of the most extreme situations imaginable. I'd be managing a staff of young employees (most of them in their 20s) and dealing with bureaucratic systems (court, police, etc.). Yes, logic screamed, "Run! Don't look back." Intuition said, "It's time. Step up." I applied and got the job.

This job was a big change. Calls came in the middle of the night. But it was always comforting to get a call in the wee hours and be totally sober and clear. Every time that happened, I was overwhelmed with gratitude for my sobriety.

There was never any true down time, because it was so hard to leave the job at the actual place of work. Despite the stress, taking this job continued to feel like the right choice. It helped me regain my confidence. Every day was stressful, yet I came home at night without the desire to take the edge off with alcohol. I learned to go straight to the meditation chair if I was too keyed up. That felt like a huge accomplishment.

The job really brought to light how many ways I seek control, and it gave me opportunities to practice the serenity prayer often. When working with teens, I had to deal with generations of dysfunction in families while also navigating the politics of government agencies. I encountered a lot of chaos and not much control.

Managing a large staff gave me many opportunities for addressing co-dependency issues. In the beginning, I was constantly trying to determine what each employee wanted and needed. I wanted to be admired and respected as a boss. But I learned I couldn't make everyone happy. Finally, I let go of trying to please everyone, and doing so provided me with yet another opportunity for growth.

Tammy Roth

HOW'D YOU DO IT

My one-year "official" sobriety date rolled around—one year since the sand dollars on the beach. This felt like an absolute miracle when I considered how long I had contemplated and struggled and how many times I had experienced a few months of sobriety only to fall off the proverbial wagon. I had heard if you could make it to the one-year mark, there was a very good chance of staying sober. I had a lot of hope.

I spent some time reflecting about my year. I had experienced a few small victories along the way. For one thing, I got my Jeep back. After 18 months, the police had located the Jeep in another county. It was returned in full working order. A man named Rabbit (a Tennessee-worthy name) had been driving it. He had apparently bought the stolen vehicle. Rabbit was a handyman and had a pile of expensive tools in the back end of the Jeep. To my delight, the police informed me I was now the proud owner of anything in the Jeep. That also included a pair of trick dice that rolled a seven or eleven every time. Things were definitely looking up.

The rectal bleeding had also stopped for a full year. Needless to say, this was a welcome change. Nothing can ruin a good day like a bloody tush, so I was happy to be free of that affliction.

I did experience a major health setback during this time, however. I lost central vision in my left eye. I had been driving with my windows down when a speck of dirt flew into my right eye. I rolled my window up and attempted to

94

clear my right eye, when I discovered I was practically blind in my left.

Holy shit!

I rushed to an eye doctor, who sent me to a retina specialist. I had a detached retina. It had occurred slowly, possibly over years, and the right eye had simply taken over. What amazing bodies we have.

I visited several doctors and learned that I could have surgery. The surgeon would insert a gas bubble into my eye. I would have to lie face down for 10 days. In my view, this was the earthly equivalent to hell. But the real downside was that there was only a small percent chance that the surgery would actually fix the problem. The retina had been detached for such a long time that the cells were probably dead and wouldn't regenerate. And there were risks to the surgery. I could end up with cataracts or other issues.

I contemplated, weighed the options and, at first, went into major fear mode. One of the doctors wanted to rush me into surgery as quickly as possible, but I trusted my intuition, which kept telling me to wait. I hoped for a miracle. Then, one day while I was meditating, I felt a wave of peace come over me, and I knew that I didn't need to do anything. I would opt out of the surgery. I would live happily with only one eye. After all, I was fortunate to have it. Perhaps if I had been younger, a teen or in my 20s, the surgery would have made more sense. The risks and miseries of the surgery were not worth the low chance of success, especially when I could see just fine to begin with. I had been living with this condition for who knows how long, and it had never caused a problem.

I have never looked back or had any fear or regret about that decision since. I don't believe I could have arrived at such a peaceful place without both sobriety and meditation. I have since had a friend point out that she was shocked at how peaceful I was about losing sight in one eye. She compared it to how absolutely nuts I had been when my

Jeep was stolen. She didn't understand how my response to both dilemmas could be so wildly different.

Serenity makes such a difference.

I celebrated the one-year anniversary at a recovery meeting. Someone asked me, "How'd you do it?"

When I looked back over my year, there were some key things that made the difference for me. I had set my ego aside, realized I didn't have all the answers and trusted the wisdom of those who had gone before me. I had let go of the belief that I was different from them, and I had fully surrendered to listening to their guidance. I knew that I couldn't get and stay sober on my own, so I trusted that the program was the right path, and for a year it had proven to be just the ticket.

Having someone to hold me accountable had proven to be highly valuable. And it was important that it was someone who understood the lure of the drink rather than my husband or a non-alcoholic friend. In those few times when I had actually contemplated drinking, the thought of having to tell Courtney was a true deterrent.

I stayed sober by really delving into the first three steps of the program along with maintaining a regimented self-care routine. I maintained the plant-based diet, continued my meditation, physical exercise and creative expression, and I went to recovery meetings.

The diet continued to be an active part of my recovery. It was a commitment to take care of my body. A whole-foods, plant-based diet combined with exercise made me feel clear and vibrant. I had also lost weight and had really healthy skin and clear eyes.

I was meditating before I gave up alcohol, but my meditation now began to have a much more profound effect in sobriety. Like most alcoholics, I have a very active (perhaps neurotic) mind. When I was drinking, it was horribly busy, and meditation helped. When I became sober, my out-of-control thoughts slowed down drastically, and I felt much more peaceful. If I don't meditate, however, my mind starts gearing itself up again. It can even kick in to high gear as it did when I drank. Sometimes my toxic thinking and obsessing actually feels like a hangover. I've heard it referred to as an emotional hangover.

When I first started meditation, I found it very difficult. I would sit for three minutes and get frustrated. I'd think it wasn't working and want to do something more productive. I could never make it past three to five minutes. Then I took a meditation class and learned some things that helped me stay focused.

First, it's important to be physically comfortable. So I sit in a chair or a sofa with my back supported. But the key for me is to not prop my head against anything. That way, if I start falling asleep, my head will bobble and wake me up. Being comfortable helps me a lot.

Second, it's not what happens during meditation but outside of meditation that counts. So even if I sit with racing thoughts and have to return to my mantra a thousand times, it's okay. I still benefit from the meditation even if it doesn't feel like it. If my mind races, it just means that I need meditation even more. And, if I fall asleep during the meditation, that's okay, too. It means I need sleep. This is how I started learning compassion for myself. I allowed these things to happen and didn't judge myself for them.

My mind is much calmer now. I have a greater sense of awareness. My reactive state has slowed down. It's as if I now have a buffer between the things that trigger me and my reaction to them. I used to blurt or lash out and then realize later what I'd said or done. Now, it's as if things are in slow motion. Something happens, I have the awareness that I'm experiencing an emotional trigger, and then I have a period of time to decide how or even *if* I'm going to react. Sometimes I don't react at all.

Now, I'm less impulsive. Prior to sobriety, the phrase "less impulsive" would have sounded boring to me, too slow, or mundane. But living in such a way actually makes me feel very awake. Eyes wide open. I know everything is okay. It's always okay.

Every meditation is different. A lot of times it's boring and seems as if time will never end. Other times, I go deep into a spacious quiet that is pure peace. Sometimes it's dreamlike. I'll be vaguely aware of a story line going on, but later, I can't really recall what it was.

I always try to practice a 20-minute meditation, but there are days when I don't make that happen, and so then I'll incorporate a shorter meditation. Even five minutes can make a difference. It's really critical that I meditate for both my sobriety and my sanity.

Meditation is how I live the second and third steps of recovery every day.

Step Two:

> *We came to believe that a power greater than ourselves could restore us to sanity.*

Meditation is my conscious action of living Step Two. I heard someone say she uses the word "clarity" instead of sanity. I like that.

Step Three:

> *We made a decision to turn our will and our lives over to the care of God as we understood him.*

Meditation is also how I turn my will over; however, I've had to reword this step to fit my beliefs. My version of the third step is:

> *I made a decision to turn my will and life over to the care of the universe.*

I believe there is a universal intelligence and it is made up of pure love and light. If I surrender and allow this energy to guide my life, it flows with ease. Meditating helps me turn down the volume on my ego and allow the universe to take the lead. A universe made of pure light and love doesn't mean that pain, suffering and other such unsavory things don't exist, as well. We must have shadow and darkness along with the light. It all exists, but meditation allows me to embrace the difficult along with the amazing.

Meditation also helps me to be much more mindful and aware in my day-to-day life. I'm able to be present and notice what I'm feeling. When I was drinking, I was constantly on the run from whatever I was feeling. I wanted to escape. With mindfulness, I don't escape anything. I feel everything. And by really feeling, by really acknowledging the truth, problems quickly dissipate. Mindfulness aligns well with the 12 steps. The saying, "This too shall pass" is a perfect example of feeling something and letting it move on.

Another thing that helped me is neurofeedback. I discovered it serendipitously. The non-profit agency where I worked received a large financial contribution that had to be used on durable medical equipment. We took this opportunity to purchase neurofeedback equipment. I went for training. In the beginning, we didn't know a lot about neurofeedback, but we had heard amazing success stories, especially in treating trauma.

Neurofeedback is brain wave training that teaches the brain and nervous system to regulate itself by making changes at a cellular level and creating new neuropathways. The result is sustainable change. It works on all symptoms the brain and central nervous system control. This includes anxiety, depression, ADD/ADHD, migraines, seizures, addiction, alcoholism, chronic pain, trauma, sleep issues, OCD, symptoms related to PMS and menopause, PTSD, high blood pressure, panic attacks and more.

Learning neurofeedback was an entirely new challenge for me. I also had the ability to perform neurofeedback on myself. When I discovered that it was helpful for recovery from alcoholism, I couldn't get enough. It took me to a new level of calm and eliminated any craving for alcohol. I loved the addition of neurofeedback to my recovery process.

For me, neurofeedback had the same effect as meditation except that it seemed much stronger and faster. It was a great supplement to the practices I already had in place. Even though I seldom had thoughts or cravings for alcohol, the neurofeedback seemed to completely obliterate any desire. I was profoundly grateful for yet another miracle in my life.

FINDING MY ART AND SOUL

I've heard that depression is unexpressed creativity. Sobriety lifted my depression, and the creativity came bursting forth. It's as if there was this big vast world just waiting for me. I had dabbled in painting in the past. I took a *Painting Made Easy* class with Whitney Freya.[3] She taught me to not be afraid of the canvas. It was very liberating. I played and explored with paint. I got a few canvases and kept painting over them. This in itself was a big step. I had so much fun and kept painting and painting.

I also enrolled in a Creative Discovery class at an artist co-op called Art & Soul.[4] I had known about Art & Soul for years. I'd driven by it. I'd visited the website. I'd received promotional emails about it. I was intrigued, but I had never been brave enough to actually check it out. I signed up for the class online and then tiptoed in on a Thursday night. I was a little nervous. I entered the space and immediately felt a creative, safe energy. The room was filled with women. There were eight of us. Men are welcome at the co-op, but none happened to be there on this first night.

The instructor asked us to "play." I was not especially good at playing. I had been a pretty serious little kid. The studio was filled to the brim with all types of items meant to make playing easy and fun. There were bins and bins of colorful cloths, yarn, bottle tops, shells, beans, glass beads,

---

[3] www.creativelyfit.com
[4] www.eartandsoul.com

keys, marbles, pompoms, shells, puzzle pieces, and more. The other women grabbed the bins and started...well, *playing*.

They built structures as if they were kids playing with Legos. I wasn't sure where to start. I found a corner and sat with my back to the group. I decided it was actually a stupid idea to have come to this place. I had an urge to bolt.

I sat facing my corner, looking at the bin full of buttons. *Should I pile buttons up in stacks of 10? Make a circle of buttons?*

I also had a jug of dried beans. I picked up this huge bin full of buttons and poured then all on top of my head. I felt silly. Ridiculous. And then I started giggling. Before I realized what I was doing, I grabbed the jug of beans and started shaking it. I was making noise.

Whohooo! I was having fun, but at the same time, I wondered if I was taking it too far.

Am I being too wild?

I contemplated reeling myself in before I got into trouble. I looked at the thousands of buttons on the floor and quickly started cleaning then up. I had made such a mess. I stopped myself and really noticed what I was feeling. I realized that I had never been much of a player as a child. This seemed like an important developmental step that I hadn't exactly mastered. I nudged my little girl self to enjoy the buttons and beans, to make a mess and make noise. Once again I found more freedom and liberation.

We continued to meet weekly. I loved this class. It felt like an incredibly safe place, free from judgment. I sensed that the other students accepted me just as I was. In the next class, we moved on to "sounding." We used our voices to scream, yodel, chant, growl, grunt, sing and laugh. Collectively we sounded like a bunch of lunatics. I learned to use my voice in ways that didn't involve trying to please someone.

Eventually, we moved on to painting. We tried activities like painting while blindfolded to separate us from our thinking minds. It's hard for your inner critic to judge your work when you can't see it. The old me, would have probably felt intimidated during this exercise. But my sober self knew that I had tapped into a critical part of my growth. I allowed myself to feel safe and connected at Art and Soul. This freedom to play, lose myself and expand is really what I was looking for in alcohol. I was always trying to lose the sense of responsibility and rigidity. And I had, along with my dignity.

Psychiatrist, Carl Jung describes addictions as "a thirst for wholeness." I was finally quenching that thirst in healthy ways and finding levels of wholeness I hadn't anticipated.

All of the activities at Art and Soul are created with the purpose of trusting our intuition, using our full mind, body and soul to create and free up the energy that can get locked inside.

I became a member of the artist co-op and I've spent hours and hours there painting and creating. I utilize the studio space frequently. I create artwork, but most of all I create the life of my dreams. The creative process flows into all aspects of my life. My life keeps expanding and expanding. Wider and deeper.

In the first year of recovery, I painted 40 abstract paintings. I went on to have an art show and sell almost half of those works. This felt like an absolute miracle. I had spent my entire life believing I wasn't artistic or even creative. I had always been terrified of anything artistic. With sobriety, I had actually become an artist.

Tapping into my creative self felt like a huge success, but I couldn't have done it without the wonderful community at the co-op. I had spent a lot of time trying to connect with others while drinking. When I drank, I dropped my guard. I used to believe that process allowed me to foster relationships. But those drunken connections were inauthentic and ultimately lacked depth. In sobriety, I have connected with strong, authentic people. I am a member of multiple groups of like-minded individuals. I have the support of a recovery community, my artist co-op, a women's circle, and I also participate in a writers meet-up. All of these forms of community have depth and meaning. There is nothing superficial about these groups. Recovery requires an immense amount of growth, and authentic connections with others have been paramount to my personal successes.

THE GOOD WIFE

Sobriety led to changes in my perspective regarding marriage. I began to recognize all the expectations and stipulations I had been putting on my relationship with Dennis. I had always assumed that a happy couple must enjoy a specific amount of activities together per week. I figured that in order to have a healthy marriage, we needed to have dinner together, attend social events together and the like.

My sobriety had changed my mentality. My growth had given me more confidence. I had also found more tools for coping with difficult situations. Through all of this, I had become less dependent on my marriage to "complete me." I had become "whole" on my own. This may sound like I was growing apart from my husband, but in fact, our marriage was actually more fulfilling. I realized that it wasn't about the quantity of time we spent together but more about the quality.

I started looking at the times in the past when I had been most frustrated with our marriage. It was usually when we were not living up to my "quota" (which only existed in my head, because I had never actually shared these lists or numbers with him). I examined how much credibility these standards actually held. I'm sure these were ideas I had picked up years ago from women's magazines or growing up with too much Mike and Carol Brady. Whatever the original source, I couldn't find any modern-day credibility to back them up.

That's when I started experimenting with my self-imposed marriage rules. First, I threw out the idea of eating dinner together. I had a totally different diet than he did. He was fine eating a can of soup or a frozen burrito, anyway. He didn't give a rip how much I enjoyed chopping and blanching broccoli. He was delighted to heat up his own processed food—I try not to judge—and sit with it in front of the TV or computer—still trying not to judge. And I was content to eat my colorful array of vegetables and grains in silence. We still talked. It just wasn't at dinnertime. We weren't missing out on anything except some outdated marriage rules.

Next I looked at how much social time we spent together. I stopped asking him to go with me to things he didn't really enjoy just because I wanted my husband by my side. And I stopped going to Titan's games. There was a time when I had thoroughly enjoyed filling my entire Sunday with tailgating, enduring weather, and screaming my drunken head off to support our Titans. But the game atmosphere wasn't resonating as much with me now that I was sober. I still like the Titans, but I don't want to devote my entire day to football. Dennis sold my season ticket. We don't do as many things together as we used to. He enjoys his sports, and I love going to retreats and workshops that involve art, writing, yoga and recovery. When we do decide to do something together, it's something we both enjoy, and that enhances the quality.

I realized I had never given Dennis space to miss me, enjoy me or truly desire me because I was always so "up in his grill" with my expectations and neediness. After I discovered a more solid connection with myself, I felt a more stable connection with him.

I used to wish he was more spiritual and would meditate or do yoga with me. I've definitely let go of that idea, and now I realize I wouldn't want him trailing me around anyway. I also know that he has his own practices that are *his* forms of meditation. He spends blissful days raking leaves, fixing the roof or installing new windows. This is meditation, too. He enjoys it. He's quiet and with himself. It's perfect for him.

MS. KNOW IT ALL

By the time I reached my two-year sobriety date, I felt like I had the whole recovery thing down. Actually, I maybe even felt a little arrogant about it, like I was more advanced than the average 12-steppers. I thought that all of my self-care, my involvement in strong communities, and the addition of neurofeedback were huge assurances that I would remain sober forever. As a two-year victory celebration, I decided I would quit going to meetings, stop thinking of myself as a recovering alcoholic and just live life as a grateful sober person.

Some underlying co-dependent thinking still resided in me. I thought it would be easier for Dennis to have a "non-drinking wife" than an alcoholic wife. Apparently, a part of me felt like damaged goods. This was all made up in my very active head. Dennis really didn't care if I was an alcoholic or a pole dancer, he just liked that I didn't drink. Regardless, I quit going to meetings to get away from what I perceived to be a negative label.

This worked out fine for a few months until we went on vacation. Dennis and I typically take the same type of vacation each year. We choose a lush setting in nature (like Lake Tahoe or the Colorado Rockies), rent a chalet, cook our own food, do a lot of hiking, and have plenty of space and quiet time. For me, this is a perfect vacation: great food, meditation, and lots of exercise. For this vacation, however, I had the grand idea that we should be spontaneous and drive down the Oregon coast without a plan. Drive until we're ready to stop each day and find a place to crash.

I discovered that spontaneous travel is not relaxing for either one of us. We were both kind of edgy. The green, eco friendly, vibe I'd heard about didn't really exist on the coast. That theme is really concentrated in the Portland area and a few other places. We discovered a lot of crappy food. I ate iceberg lettuce salads and processed veggie burgers. This was not my happy view of a plant-based diet. Because we slept in hotels and at a different place every night, I let meditation go out the window. I didn't feel like I had a space devoted to my practice. I also couldn't find any opportunities to hike. We had some beach walks, but the weather was cold, rainy and windy.

On the third night, we stayed in a Jacuzzi suite at a lovely beachfront hotel. All of the stress and the lack of self-care had warped my grateful, sober brain. Suddenly, I felt that I needed a glass of wine to go with that Jacuzzi. I was convinced it would not be a problem. After all, I was just a grateful sober person. I had conveniently forgotten that I was an alcoholic and that just one sip would trigger an entire disease.

Dennis was my grounding force. As I stood looking at the wine aisle in the grocery store, rationalizing why it was a good idea, he put his hand on the small of my back and said, "Come on. You don't want to give up all your sober time." He gently guided me to the nearby aisle of chips.

Fine. I didn't get the wine, but I was determined to do *something* bad. I loaded up on junk food and also got a six-pack of O'Doul's, which is dangerous. I was pissed. I stomped out of the grocery store like a toddler. The first thing I saw was a car with a vanity license plate that only had two letters on it. "AA." Enough said.

When I got home I took myself to a meeting, and it was such a sweet reminder of all that is magical about a support system. I knew then that I must maintain a recovery community. I need that constant reminder that I'm not just a sober person. I really am an alcoholic, and the bitch will kill me if given the opportunity.

I also realized I needed to be there, not just for me, but for others, as well. The text even states that it's imperative to work with others. A key aspect to recovery is giving back. I started thinking about how I might best serve other recovering alcoholics, especially women in recovery, beyond just being present at meetings and offering to be a sponsor. I sensed there was a specific calling for me.

LOSING STEAM

I had been the director of the Crisis Shelter for two years when I started losing motivation. I kept trying to rally and convince myself I just needed a vacation or a new hair color. Something to switch things up. But I was actually feeling burnt out. And that pissed me off. I didn't want to have to figure out the professional thing again. My instinct was to run. Fast. I wanted to get away from the uncomfortable feeling. I wished I could just quit showing up for work.

I realized this had become a pattern for me. When things got uncomfortable, I bolted. The familiar instinct had shown itself again, but this time I wanted to deal with it constructively rather than impulsively.

I went to a few therapy sessions to see if I could dig into the root issues associated with my tendency to bolt. I had a memory from when I was 4 years old. I was in the front yard with a group of older boys who were hiding in the ditch. They were planning to ambush a couple of other boys by throwing rocks at them when they rode by on their bikes. I decided to join the party. I picked up one rock and lobbed it toward the road. I apparently had a stout little 4-year-old arm. I popped a boy in the head. He had to go to the hospital for stitches. At home, I earned a rather severe spanking for my actions. I was shocked that this memory came up in my therapy session. My self-talk associated with the memory was, "I always mess things up." I had messed it up for the boys in the ditch, I had messed it up for the boy I dinged and I had messed up my day up by picking up that

111

stupid rock. I wanted to get the heck out of that situation that day. That was the start of wanting to escape when things got uncomfortable.

But wanting to escape is simply a normal feeling. It's common among alcoholics as well as among people without substance addictions. We don't like to feel uncomfortable. That is why we are essentially a society full of people with addictions. We can't put our smartphones down, for example. We have cravings for sugar and carbs. We take lots of prescription meds. We just don't want to endure negative feelings.

I told my boss how I was feeling about the job, but I also assured her that I wasn't going to jump ship. I told her that I hoped there was a way for me to remain at the agency but not have so much intense responsibility. She was amenable. Each time we met, we talked about possibilities, and she always checked in with how overwhelmed I felt. Having the opportunity to talk about it rather than escape it was very empowering.

I hung in there and stayed at the job. I felt confident that I was breaking a pattern. I fully experienced the discomfort of not enjoying my job anymore but not quitting. I acknowledged the discomfort and decided it wouldn't kill me. And it didn't.

HAPPY BUDDHA

I began attending a recovery meeting in Nashville that was based on Buddhist principles. We would meditate for 20 minutes, and then a facilitator would speak for 20 minutes, and then we had 20 minutes of discussion. I loved this meeting. It felt like the next stage of recovery for me. I loved being surrounded by people in recovery who also meditated. I volunteered as a facilitator of the group and felt very connected to this type of service. As time went on, I started realizing I connected with the meditation part of the meeting, but I wasn't Buddhist, so I felt a bit like an imposter each time I attended. I also really missed my "women's only" meetings.

I kept wishing for a women's meditation recovery group, until finally it dawned on me that I could start one myself. I advertised and sent flyers out to friends in recovery as well as to local therapists. I advertised for about three weeks prior to starting, and on the first night of the meeting, eight women showed up. It was lovely. The meeting has continued ever since, with attendance never falling off.

Group volunteers share the facilitation responsibilities. It involves reading our preamble, which states that we respect all forms of recovery and are not a substitution for any other program. The facilitator leads us in five minutes of guided meditation and then we have 15 minutes of silence. The remaining 40 minutes are reserved for open discussion, the same as any other 12-step meeting.

TIME FOR A CHANGE

My life was extremely peaceful. Except for work. I had sat with the discomfort all summer. I was still running the shelter, but I knew that it was time for something to shift. I had managed to not flee and had endured the restlessness, but now it really *was* time for change. I put a plea out to the universe.

During the fall equinox, I attended a retreat facilitated by Joan Borysenko. I went into the weekend with the intention of finding clarity about my next step. On Saturday morning, all 30 attendees crowded into a sweat lodge. The sweat lodge ceremony is a Native American tradition to promote physical detoxification, emotional purification and spiritual connection. The ceremony takes place in a dark structure made of willows and blankets. This is the lodge.

A ceremonial fire keeper builds a fire outside of the lodge and heats stones. He or she then brings the stones one by one into the lodge and pours water onto them in order to fill the space with hot steam. It's intense. Hot yoga doesn't hold a candle to a good old sweat lodge. On this particular weekend, it was hot outside, and it was damn hot inside that little tent where we all crouched on the ground for what seemed like three hours.

I felt fine. I even felt a little sense of superiority, I suppose, because I was able to crouch and sweat without a problem. By the fourth round, I felt differently. This was the dumbest idea I had ever heard of. And I was sure I was about to have a psychotic break. I imagined myself suddenly

screaming and thrashing around, destroying the te
knocking people in the head with hot stones. But
glanced over, remembering I was crouching knee
with wise woman Joan, and it would behoove me to act
sane. I also realized I was struggling big time with feeling
uncomfortable. I had triggered my friend the amygdala and
the fight or flight instinct. The facilitator said we must feel
uncomfortable for change to occur. That put everything into
perspective, and I was suddenly able to not only tolerate my
discomfort but also to welcome it.

During this weekend I identified another thought pattern
that was currently holding me back. I had been thinking, "I
should stay put, be satisfied and grateful for my job."

Should. Should. Should.

I was ready to break this pattern. The internal message
was that I was getting too big for my britches and I should
be grateful and content. "Should" was a word others had
used to caution me in the past when I had vowed to make
changes. I recognized the messaging in regards to leaving my
first marriage, leaving the corporate jobs, getting out of
Clarksville, etc. None of these things were actually horrible,
but if I had stayed with any of them I would have been
settling for less. Looking back, I am grateful that I eventually
cast off the "shoulds." It was time for me to do that again.

At the retreat, our next activity was zip lining. This was
supposed to work as a metaphor for how we live life. I
volunteered to go first and quickly jumped off the ramp
before I even knew all the safety rules. Off I went, flying
through the trees. I eventually crashed head on into the
guide at the other end. On my next turn, I slowed it down
by putting on the brakes. I tried being more intentional, but
the damn thing went way too slow, and I got stuck midway.
The guide had to lasso me in. Apparently the key was to
somehow lean back and let the zip line carry you. Allowing
myself to be carried continues to be one of my biggest areas
of resistance.

At the end of the retreat, I felt open to whatever might occur with my job. I promised myself to allow the change to unfold instead of bulldozing my way into something that wouldn't be the right fit. I also fully committed to listening and responding to intuition and inspiration.

By Monday morning, I had received a text message from my boss. Over the next few months I would begin offering neurofeedback to the general public to create a revenue stream for the crisis center. This was the start of a new opportunity for me, and I was thrilled with the possibilities.

LAYERS AND LAYERS

As I moved into the new year, I continued to feel gratitude for all that was right in my life. I did, however, decide to take things up a notch. It was not unusual for me to minimize most things about my success. I made the commitment that the next year would be a colorful coming out party for my true being. I would allow myself to shine.

I wanted to play a larger role in life. Sometimes I pretended I was an actress playing a vivacious character. In those moments I would become more animated, louder and more colorful than usual. I doubt that anyone really noticed the difference, but I felt like I was breaking out of an old pattern. It was a fun approach.

I started working with a creativity coach, Jackie Schlicher of Visions Manifest Coaching[5], to see what else I might be able to coax out of myself. The topic of writing kept coming up. Finally, in one session, I addressed the fact that I knew she wanted me to write a memoir, but I wasn't sure that I was ready.

She quickly let me know that she had never brought it up, but that I had brought it up in every single session. *Really?* Well, that was a bit embarrassing. *What kind of denial was I living in?* My soul was calling me out to write the story, and obviously I had some real resistance to it.

I had purposely chosen Jackie as my coach because she was what I would call a "mother-earth-badass-don't-really-

[5] www.visionsmanifest.com

care-what-you-think-of-me creative midwife." I figured she would stand up to my resistance and not sugarcoat anything. We launched into an exercise.

She asked why I was considering writing my memoir. In hindsight, I know the purpose of the conversation was to push my buttons and get me to own my process. She questioned why I thought I was good enough to write my story. She kept pushing, and I grew more and more irritated. Finally I screamed, "I don't know if I am writing it or not! But if I do, and it helps one person, than it will be worth it. And maybe that one person will only be me. But it will still be worth it. By God, I am writing this memoir. So there!"

Jackie just smiled. She wasn't fighting me. I was the only one fighting myself. I committed to writing the story and set a deadline to finish it.

In March, I was invited to do an art show. The show would consist of the 40 abstracts I had painted during my first year of recovery. In my mind, this officially made me feel like an artist. My life was exploding with creativity and excitement.

Gulp.

I felt a little nervous when things were so good. Oddly, sometimes there is discomfort in total comfort. I had spent my entire life seeking comfort and trying to change things. Being in a place of contentedness suddenly felt very foreign. I was used to a buzz of anxiety, a little bit of chaos, a drop or two of drama.

I named my art show *Answering the Call*. The signature piece for the show was titled, "Woman of Wisdom." The Art and Soul co-op had helped me find the strength to shine. I asked members of the art co-op and my women's circle to participate in the event. Many performed music with original songs they had written. They were all women who were exploring their own creativity. None of us were professional artists or musicians, simply women on a creative journey. When it came time to speak to the crowd, I nearly burst into tears. I felt incredibly vibrant, and alive and I no longer needed the calming effects of alcohol.

I told the crowd about a book, *The Millionth Circle: How to Change Ourselves and the World: The Essential Guide to Women's Circles*, by Jean Shinoda Bolen[6]. The book expresses the idea that every time people have an intentional gathering, whether it be a circle or an offering of creativity, we are essentially putting an offering of love out to the universe. And from that, there is a ripple effect. I asked the people present to carry that little ripple of hope, joy and creativity out into their communities. It was a beautiful night, and I sold 18 of the 40 paintings. My creative process had been to put on layers of paint and then use a palette knife to scrape off layers. This process allowed the light from underneath to shine through. It felt very symbolic of my recovery. I was excavating something beautiful in my life and on the canvas.

---

[6] Bolen, Jean Shinoda. *The Millionth Circle: How to Change Ourselves and the World: The Essential Guide to Women's Circles*. Berkeley, CA: Conari, 1999. Print.

HOW SWEET IT IS

As I approached my fourth year of recovery, I also began working Step Four.

We made a searching and fearless moral inventory of ourselves.

I had been slow going through the steps because I'd been slowly breaking down my ego. The text says it's the destruction of self-centeredness. Plus, I wasn't used to doing anything slowly, so it was another new approach to life. The 12 steps can be worked at any pace. Many people go through them quickly when they first get into recovery and keep going back through them over and over. There's no particular timetable to work through them. For me, going slow seemed very important.

In the beginning, I thought I knew best and didn't fully follow the program protocol, but as time went on and I picked up the text here and there, I kept seeing more and more of the brilliance in it. As I did this searching and fearless moral inventory, I was gaining awareness of my arrogance. I've always had very strong opinions about most things. I've always insisted on doing things my way. And that's pretty much how I had done recovery...my way. I first tried it without a recovery program, which didn't work. Then I went the program route, but I always believed I was just a bit different than the average recovering alcoholic. This isn't such an unusual trait in alcoholics. Most of us don't like to follow rules.

As I listed resentments, almost all came back to resenting myself for what I did or didn't do in each situation. I definitely recognized a pattern that I had developed when I divorced of rebellion, being a know-it-all, and not liking to follow rules or protocol. In sobriety, I have become a lot less rebellious, and I enjoy feeling much calmer and less antagonistic.

While doing this searching and fearless moral inventory, I had a dream that there was a huge bear at my front door. I ran to the door and reached out to touch the bear. "Hello, Bear!" I said. "What is your message for me?" Then, suddenly I jumped back, realizing I should be afraid of the bear. Yet I was so drawn to the bear. I knew she was bringing me a gift of wisdom, but logic kicked in again and told me to back away.

When I awoke and examined the dream, it felt like a dance between my mystical self and my mainstream self that conforms to societal norms. When I looked up the symbolism of the bear in the book *Animal Speak: The Spiritual & Magical Powers of Creatures Great & Small* by Ted Andrews[7], the part of the message that most resonated with me was the bear's affinity for honey. Perhaps she was there to help me get in touch with the sweetness of life. I liked this idea.

The next day I went to an iridologist. I was seeking alternative healing for two health issues that had plagued me for years. I was frustrated. I had made a lifelong commitment to a whole-foods, plant-based diet and an overall healthy lifestyle, so I have to admit that I was quite miffed that I didn't actually have perfect health. I struggled with sinus and constipation issues. Mainstream doctors had suggested antihistamines for the sinus troubles and told me

---

[7] Bolen, Jean Shinoda. *The Millionth Circle: How to Change Ourselves and the World: The Essential Guide to Women's Circles.* Berkeley, CA: Conari, 1999. Print.

not worry about going to the bathroom every day. But I wanted to find a solution. Over the years, I tried acupuncture, colonics, chiropractic care, energy healing and more. These alternative healing methods helped, but nothing completely solved the problem. So there I was at the iridologist, trying yet another route. An iridologist examines a magnified view of the iris, where hundreds of thousands of nerves and energy flows connect with every tissue and organ of the body. Disease will show up in the iris before it actually manifests elsewhere.

The iridologist told me I had a massive candida overgrowth full of fungus and parasites in my gut. She asked if I had a sugar addiction.

"No," I said.

She looked at me with very skeptical eyes. She said this overgrowth feeds on sugar and yeast, and it looked like I had been indulging in massive sugar consumption for years.

"Um, well, I did abuse alcohol for two decades," I said.

That was the problem. But I offered that I'd been sober for almost four years. Apparently, that didn't matter. I'd fed the beasties for too long and they had multiplied. She asked if I had also been on a lot of antibiotics. Antibiotics kill the good bacteria in the gut, allowing the bad to take over even more.

I hardly ever went to the doctor, let alone took medications. But then I remembered my meningitis episode. I had been pumped full of antibiotics for three days straight. Candida is very hard to kill. It takes dedication to an herbal regime to first kill the nasties and then even more dedication to adhere to a strict diet that keeps the bad bacteria at bay while good flora repopulates the gut. I was committed.

The arsenal of herbal supplements seemed manageable. The diet was rigid. No starches or sugars, or gluten, or soy, or beans, or dairy, or caffeine, or artificial sweeteners and on and on—for three to six months. One slip up could undo weeks of work. It was a lot like getting sober. No slip ups. I couldn't have one chocolate kiss or even a piece of gum because it would reactivate the candida. It was intense, but again, I was so happy to have an answer that I was willing to give it a try.

It felt like the work was also really connected to Step Four. I was clearing out my psychic shame closet and then I got to clear out my toxic, cesspool of a gut, too. Yes, it definitely felt like a new layer of clearing. I intuitively knew that by clearing out both toxic waste sites I would be getting in touch with a far sweeter aspect of life. I thanked the bear for her message.

AND YET ANOTHER LAYER

My new diet revealed another level of addiction. For the first three days, I kept finding my hand reaching for things like dark chocolate, granola, or a piece of gum.

I discovered I had this "reward system" in place for myself throughout the day. It was usually just a bite, but there were a lot of bites by the end of the day. This cleanse really forced me to be mindful about what I was doing. When I felt like treating myself, I instead tuned into the moment and allowed myself to feel gratitude. It was a wonderful shift. I recognized that I was always seeking something external instead of basking in what already existed.

I read a book called *The Body Ecology Diet: Recovering Your Health and Rebuilding Your Immunity* by Donna Gates and Linda Shatz[8]. They write:

> *Alcoholics usually have candida that has spread to the liver and as a result, experience powerful cravings from the overgrowth of yeast organisms AND an addiction to sugar and more alcohol. If you have candida, you may find yourself drawn to sugary foods and alcohol, so it's not surprising that many alcoholics turn to carbohydrate-rich food when they stop drinking.*

---

[8] Gates, Donna, and Linda Schatz. *The Body Ecology Diet: Recovering Your Health and Rebuilding Your Immunity.* Carlsbad, CA: Hay House, 2011. Print.

She recommends cutting out sugar and starches and consuming at least two cups of coconut Kefir per day to eliminate sugar and alcohol cravings. I remember consuming a lot of chocolate and soy lattes in my early sobriety.

Within just a few days of doing this cleanse, I began to feel relief from my symptoms. At the one-month mark, the symptoms were 99 percent gone. In order to ensure that I was healed and that good bacteria instead of bad bacteria remained in control of my belly, I still needed to adhere to a strict diet.

I also had to rethink my vegan lifestyle. Enzymes found in meat were important for my digestive system. I knew I wasn't going to go back to consuming dairy; that would only aggravate my sinuses. But I had to think about eating meat again. This was a difficult decision. I had felt so good about embracing a plant-based diet, knowing that I was not contributing to the mistreatment of animals. I was not supporting factory farms. My body needed meat, however. I had been doing it a disservice by pumping my system so full of carb-heavy beans in search of protein. I had contributed to the candida. After much thought, I decided I needed to do what was right for my body. I now choose meat that's raised on local and sustainable farms and is grass fed, cage free, etc.

Through these diet changes, I discovered what a distraction food had been. It was actually very similar to alcohol, and I had never realized it. I was always preoccupied with when I would next eat and always counting calories in my head and calculating how much I had burned at yoga or a boot camp class. The new diet eliminated cravings and therefore my preoccupation. The new diet also gave me appreciation for the uniqueness of each person's body chemistry. Listening to your own body is key. There is a lot of information out there and it can be incredibly confusing. Listening to the wisdom of your own system is the answer to finding a diet optimal to your health.

EMBRACING VULNERABILITY

As I dove into writing this memoir, I also had to come to terms with vulnerability. I felt multiple layers of fear when it came to sharing my experience.

What if people thought I was a crappy writer? Yes, some people would definitely think I was a crappy writer. And what about being a therapist and admitting that I had also been a drunk?

Gulp!

That was really opening myself up to judgment. I looked back over the ethical guidelines for professional counseling and felt confident I had been ethical, but I had to come to terms with the fact that others would definitely judge me. What would the people whom I had been in recovery with think? I also wondered about family, friends and colleagues—people who knew me in general. Would they question my perception of life? Would they wonder why I had left out certain aspects? Oh, and there was also the risk that not one single person would give a damn about what I had written.

Ouch.

The process presented a lot of potential for disaster, but I decided I was willing to take those risks. Another strong reason that I wanted to get the story out was that, on one hand, I understood and respected the anonymous part of recovery and how so many people need it to feel safe in their process. But on the other hand, secrecy feels like a hot bed for breeding shame. I did not want to approach my recovery in a way that was hiding or playing small.

I want to always be out and available to anyone who might be interested in the same approach.

I also want to help take some of the stigma out of the disease of alcoholism. I want to be another face of alcoholism. I'm just an ordinary middle-age woman who has achieved some degree of success in her life. But I'm also a flaming alcoholic—gratefully recovering—but alcoholic all the same. Perhaps my story will inspire others on their own roads to recovery.

When I look at my journey over the past five years, there has been a lot of trial and error, two steps forward and one back. I know the journey never ends. What I believe now will be very different in the next five years.

For me to find success in sobriety, I needed and continue to need a traditional recovery program combined with many other tools. I believe the traditional recovery program saved my life and gave me hope. The program continues to provide me with a solid structure and also a community of people who truly get me. Exploring my creativity and practicing yoga and meditation has also helped me uncover rich gifts. These practices have offered me a life I never dreamed possible. I continue to delve deeper and deeper into the creative, pulsing, juicy world in which I now live.

This is true recovery—recovering parts of myself that had atrophied and withered. I have bloomed into full color, and for that I am profoundly grateful.

If I were to begin listing all of the phenomenal people who have come into my life over the years and inspired, nudged, believed in, accepted, and assisted me on my path, then: first, I would be sure to leave someone out; and second, you would probably get bored reading all of the names. If you are reading this book, and you know me, you have touched my life in some way. I thank you from the bottom of my heart.

RESOURCES

About the Author

To learn more about recovery-based meditation groups and retreats, visit www.tammyroth.com.

Books

Andrews, Ted. *Animal-speak: The Spiritual & Magical Powers of Creatures Great & Small.* St. Paul, MN, U.S.A.: Llewellyn Publications, 1993. Print.

Bolen, Jean Shinoda. *The Millionth Circle: How to Change Ourselves and the World: The Essential Guide to Women's Circles.* Berkeley, CA: Conari, 1999. Print.

Covington, Stephanie. *A Woman's Way through the Twelve Steps.* Center City, MN: Hazelden, 1994. Print.

Gates, Donna, and Linda Schatz. *The Body Ecology Diet: Recovering Your Health and Rebuilding Your Immunity.* Carlsbad, CA: Hay House, 2011. Print.

Walsch, Neale Donald. *Conversations with God: An Uncommon Dialogue.* New York: G.P. Putnam's Sons, 1996. Print.

Links

Art and Soul Co-op, www.eartandsoul.com

Freya, Whitney, Creatively Fit, www.creativelyfit.com

Schlicher, Jackie, Visions Manifest Coaching, www.visionsmanifest.com

AN EXCERPT
New Bottom — Turning the Other Cheek

I had heard in the recovery world that when I reached five years of sobriety I should listen for a loud thump because it would be the sound of my head falling out of my ass. I always met this bit of homespun recovery wisdom with a smug smile.

Not me!

I had such a strong foundation of self-awareness and insight in my recovery. What more was there to learn about myself?

And then it happened. I celebrated five years of sobriety, and not only did I hear the thump, I felt its reverberation through my soul. My head, indeed, fell out of my ass.

When I was fifty, I was five years sober, and I discovered I had spent a lifetime numbing, ignoring, rationalizing, and most of all, minimizing the less-than-idyllic environment in which I had grown up. I'd never had the desire to see myself as a victim, and I avoided others who exhibited a victim mentality. Come to think of it, I wasn't too fond of vulnerability either. I had spent the majority of my life being stoic, strong, and resilient—my defense mechanisms. But the truth is that I grew up in a home filled with dysfunction and a little body filled with fear.

What did it mean to have my head fall out of my ass? I chose to view my experience as an exciting journey of learning to live a life filled with authenticity and vulnerability. I believed I had a solid handle on authenticity. But authenticity is not always a pretty thing. When I was a kid, my family worked hard to look freshly washed and cleanly pressed in the eyes of the rest of the community. So as an adult, I vowed to always keep it real. I thought I was keeping it real by *not* putting on a crisp façade of perfection.

I am not the person who can turn the world on with her smile. To this day, people tell me that the look on my face speaks volumes about how I feel. I cannot deny when I'm shocked, appalled, or insulted. Poker has never been in the cards for me. The look on my face matches what's going on inside. In the past, I rarely had a smile on my face, because I was rarely happy.

When I was a graduate student studying to be a therapist, an enthusiastic classmate invited me out for a drink. She asked, "Why are you so aloof?" In my old habit of assuming everything was about me, I imagined that she and all of my other classmates had sat around together over coffee psychoanalyzing my underlying issues. I was appalled that she would ask me this question. I didn't know I was unhappy, and I didn't view myself as aloof. I thought I was simply an introvert, and therefore, if I was a little reserved, I was just being my authentic self.

In my corporate career, I had learned about the Myers-Briggs Personality Types and was thrilled to discover the rationale for why I was so withdrawn. I liked finally having the introvert label instead of just being viewed as inadequate. With time, however, I discovered introversion actually has nothing to do with authenticity.

Even though I wasn't yet sober, as a young corporate woman, I craved journeying within to understand myself. Exploring my introversion was an exciting beginning because I had no inner life to speak of. I didn't know who I was on a deep level. I tightly defended and protected my perceived authenticity. My sobriety and recovery are all about discovering my authentic self.

I recognize that I am still an introvert, but I'm no longer aloof—or sullen or sour for that matter—because I'm happy, inside and out.

And my authenticity is slowly but consistently coming out of hiding. Looks can still sometimes be deceiving. My face has been locked into a scowl, so I have to consciously remind myself to smile. When I was a kid, I often heard the accusations, "what are *you* smiling about?" or "wipe that smile off your face." I discovered early that it was safer to be blank and invisible. Now I am retraining my brain and my nervous system that it is safe to be seen, and the newfound happiness is showing up on my face.

***

When I learned that my alcoholism links to my upbringing and that I needed to explore my past in order to understand the connection, the idea exhausted and overwhelmed me. Hadn't I done all the work just getting sober? Getting sober took grit, will, and some vulnerability. These next steps would require looking at, exploring, and acknowledging my past; determining how it informed my present; and making the necessary changes for a healthier future. As Maya Angelou said, "I hadn't so much forgotten as I couldn't bring myself to remember."

Remembering was a big task. But a very important one.

Ultimately, it changed how I live my life. Living from this core self has allowed me to create deeper levels of intimacy in all of my relationships. However, not everyone who was here at the beginning chose to stay.

57628294R00077

Made in the USA
Lexington, KY
20 November 2016